"*She's the One* is frank, feisty, and laugh-out-loud funny."

—Sue Shapiro, author of
Lighting Up and *Five Men Who Broke My Heart*

"Greg opens the door to the male mind and tells it like it is. Being 'the one' is about being your fabulous, sexy, lusty self, and Greg leads you down that path with humor, humility, his own embarrassing stories, and, most of all, honesty. It had me laughing out loud."

—Rachel Kramer Bussel, columnist, *The Village Voice*

"Finally, an advice book that depicts men as people you'd actually want to date. . . . Greg's funny and positive advice should help couples get, and stay, together for all the right reasons."

—Lynn Harris, columnist,
Glamour magazine, and cocreator of BreakupGirl.net

"Who knew men were so humble, tuned in, and—gasp—vulnerable? Thanks to Gilderman's painfully honest and, at times, laugh-out-loud funny take on sex and dating, single women everywhere can take heart. Men are just as hungry for companionship (and of course good sex) as we women are."

—Elise Abrams Miller, author of *Star Craving Mad*

"In these pages, Greg untangles the inner workings of my boyfriends past and husband present. What an insightful read."

—Kristen Kemp, author of *Breakfast at Bloomingdale's*

She's the One

the One

The Surprising Truth About
What Makes a Woman
a Keeper

Gregory
Gilderman

A Perigee Book

A PERIGEE BOOK
Published by the Penguin Group
Penguin Group (USA) Inc.
375 Hudson Street, New York, New York 10014, USA
Penguin Group (Canada), 90 Eglinton Avenue East, Suite 700, Toronto, Ontario M4P 2Y3, Canada
(a division of Pearson Penguin Canada Inc.)
Penguin Books Ltd., 80 Strand, London WC2R 0RL, England
Penguin Group Ireland, 25 St. Stephen's Green, Dublin 2, Ireland (a division of Penguin Books Ltd.)
Penguin Group (Australia), 250 Camberwell Road, Camberwell, Victoria 3124, Australia
(a division of Pearson Australia Group Pty. Ltd.)
Penguin Books India Pvt. Ltd., 11 Community Centre, Panchsheel Park, New Delhi—110 017, India
Penguin Group (NZ), Cnr. Airborne and Rosedale Roads, Albany, Auckland 1310, New Zealand
(a division of Pearson New Zealand Ltd.)
Penguin Books (South Africa) (Pty.) Ltd., 24 Sturdee Avenue, Rosebank, Johannesburg 2196, South Africa

Penguin Books Ltd., Registered Offices: 80 Strand, London WC2R 0RL, England

While the author has made every effort to provide accurate telephone numbers and Internet addresses at
the time of publication, neither the publisher nor the author assumes any responsibility for errors, or for
changes that occur after publication. Further, the publisher does not have any control over and does not
assume any responsibility for author or third-party websites or their content.

Some names and identifying traits have been changed. Some quotes have been edited for clarity.

First edition: January 2007

Library of Congress Cataloging-in-Publication Data

Gilderman, Gregory.
    She's the one / Gregory Gilderman.
      p. cm.
    ISBN-13 978-0-399-53300-6
    1. Man-woman relationships.   2. Mate selection.   I. Title.
    HQ801.G445   2007
    646.7'7—dc22   2006049493

PRINTED IN THE UNITED STATES OF AMERICA

10 9 8 7 6 5 4 3 2 1

Most Perigee Books are available at special quantity discounts for bulk purchases for sales promotions,
premiums, fund-raising, or educational use. Special books, or book excerpts, can also be created to fit
specific needs. For details, write: Special Markets, The Berkley Publishing Group, 375 Hudson Street,
New York, New York 10014.

For Jessica

ACKNOWLEDGMENTS

I'd like to thank the editors who have been kind enough to publish my work over the past few years: Meaghan Buchan, Judy Dutton, Ann Gonsalves, Marina Khidekel, Jeff Koyen, the wonderful Marian Lizzi of Penguin, Mark Moore, Catherine New, Dorothy Robinson, Ron Varrial, and Kate White. I also thank Miriam Parker, colleague and friend, without whose encouragement, editorial insights, and occasional willingness to pick up the tab, neither I nor this book would exist. I love you all.

CONTENTS

She's the One

Introduction

Why I Wrote This Book

Let's start with a confession.

I'm a straight white male who writes for women's magazines. My best friend installs kitchens, my father teaches college students sociology, I tell millions of women whether to give it up on the third date. It's a strange job but I'm honored to have it.

Since we're being honest, let me share a thought about women's magazines. They're fun to read and fun to write for, but when it comes down to it, most of what they publish about men ranges from shallow to useless.

I'm thinking not only of sex tips not many guys would actually enjoy ("Probe him with your finger and give him a prostate massage!" appeared in one magazine not long ago), but of the generic "guy" who is the object of articles like "How to Please Your Guy," "How to Cook for Your Guy," "1,000 Sexual Positions for Your Guy," etc. That "guy" is the "guy's guy" of a beer commercial: simple, stupid, and interested only in how you look or what goes on in bed.

Sound familiar? It should. The idea pervades just about every self-help book or pop-advice piece ever written: men are visual; men are from Mars; men only think of pizza, football, getting laid, or some way to enjoy all three at once.

There's truth to that stereotype, but it's also true that men can feel vulnerable, have insecurities, fall in love, enjoy romance, and have every other feeling your average talk show or magazine pretends doesn't exist in the male emotional repertoire.

The U.S. Census estimates that almost 90 percent of American men will be married at least once by the age of forty. If you subtract guys who are gay, high school dropouts, or convicted felons, it's probably around 100 percent. Men take vows, make babies, buy minivans, and utter "I love you" despite there being more opportunities for casual hooking up than at any other time in history. Do you know why this is?

It's because we want to.

Every guy is looking for the One. And what men want from her is the obvious stuff—love, honesty, friendship, and fidelity—but also *that she meets some distinctly male needs.*

What are those needs? That's what this book is about. It's about what we're thinking when we decide a girl we happen to be dating is someone we want to spend a very long time with, possibly in a jointly owned minivan and bi-level suburban house. It's about falling in love.

Like most guys, I never gave this kind of emotional stuff much thought—until I received a phone call one afternoon from my editor at *Cosmopolitan* magazine.

The Call That Changed It All

"Write something about how a girl can boost a guy's ego," she told me. "I hear guys need that more than sex."

I'd been writing for the magazine for a few months, so I knew the drill. I'd call or email every guy I knew and ask each of them—as I had in the past about "Secret Sex Fears!" and "First-Date Red Flags!"—to give me some quotes. I'd pick the funniest four stories, change the names, blaze through five hundred words the day the piece was due, then wait three or four months till the column was published, likely in an issue with an airbrushed Avril Lavigne on the cover. (Remember her?)

But a funny thing happened on this assignment. *The guys actually liked the topic.* They opened up. They got emotional. That is, rather than ridicule me for writing for a publication that features perfume ads, relationship quizzes, and the ever-popular Guy Without His Shirt, they gave me honest answers.

They talked about moments when the women in their lives had made them feel important and appreciated when life was making them feel small. How a compliment about his prowess in bed had stayed with him for years. How the moment he knew his girlfriend was the One wasn't when she wore a sexy dress or was having a great hair day—it was when she said an especially kind word or did something that, taken out of context, might seem like it had been lifted out of a bad romance novel, like telling him out of the blue that she loves and admires him.

These guys were telling me something that became more and more clear as I kept asking questions: that the criteria men use for serious girlfriends are much, much different from what they use for short-term flings, and that almost everyone in the relationship-writing business seems to focus on the former instead of the latter.

Think about it. All those articles about wearing this kind of skirt or having this kind of jeans or those kinds of nails are pretty much focusing on men's desire for physical beauty. And, of course, there's no relationship if there's no sexual attraction, so that kind of advice is important.

But what's unsaid is that when a guy is looking for a woman for a long-term relationship, her character and her values become extremely important. The truth is, no matter how often you see the man-as-fratboy in movies or on television, most men have a life goal of settling down with one terrific girl.

Now if you've ever read *Cosmo*, you know my editor wasn't looking for a book-length treatise on what makes a man love a woman. She wanted something light, and that's what I gave her. But as the weeks went by, I couldn't help thinking there was an idea here worth writing more about. Namely, that *what makes a guy view a girl as marriage or serious girlfriend material is her character.*

This got me thinking about my own life.

From Chaos to Calm

In the spring of 2002, I was at the apex of my dating phase.[1] I'd been hosting a show on Manhattan public access television for about three years, and it had turned my life into a state of gloriously sordid chaos.

Now let me tell you about this show, because I've been interviewed about it and I've always hedged a bit on what the story is.

The show was created to improve my love life. For years I had observed what I like to call the Keith Richards Effect.

_____

1. This had been preceded by my rather long "getting rejected" phase.

That is, if you take a normal guy—in his case, a bedraggled freak with the pulse rate of Walt Disney postcryogenic freeze—and put him in a rock band, on a stage, on television, or in a movie, he suddenly becomes irresistible to women.

There are exceptions. Ernest Borgnine comes to mind. But then again, so does Larry King. Do you think he'd have that same hot, young wife if he were Larry the Tire Salesman? Of course not. It's the very fact of being a part of a glamorous and powerful medium that makes him attractive.

I wanted a piece of this.

So in December 2001, I applied for a show at Manhattan Neighborhood Network (MNN), Manhattan's public access television station, and was given my own live talk show on Channel 56, Wednesdays at 11:30 p.m. I called it *Mr. Greg Live*.

Here Come the Ladies

Now, the ladies of New York City didn't give a crap about Gregory Gilderman, comedian/temp, but they sure as hell seemed to like Mr. Greg. After a few shows, I was being invited out on dates, to parties, out for drinks, and even right to a hotel room by a makeup artist visiting from Los Angeles.

All this was made far easier by the fact that the topic of

every show was my horrible love life. I also posted my email address and phone number on the screen for the length of every show, which I'm sure didn't hurt. And I'd usually begin the program—and *program* is a rather strong word given that the show was just a close-up of my head while I took phone calls—by saying something like, "Well, hard as it may be to believe, I'm still single."

Like I said: sordid. Not Led Zeppelin circa 1971 sordid, but pretty bad for a guy who normally spent his Saturday nights renting films like *I, Claudius*.

Anyway. Like Rick James on *Behind the Music*, I reveled in and misspent my riches. My relationships with these viewers were fleeting, and most of my waking hours were spent feeling a combination of loneliness, failure, and depression.

I mentioned before that I was a temp. My bosses would invariably catch the show, so I'd be told things like, "Would you mind FedExing this, Mr. Greg?"

I was also a comedian. What kind of comedian? The kind that makes no money. The only income I ever derived from show business was from organizing amateur comedy shows at a Greenwich Village club called the Comedy Cellar. And it was no booster of the ol' self-esteem to watch first-timers from those shows have their careers fly past mine. (My most famous alum: *Saturday Night Live*'s Andy Samberg. Very cool guy.)

To sum up, my life consisted of three elements: career

failure, casual sex, and faxing. The second of those was so good I deluded myself into thinking I could go on living that way for quite a while.

And then everything changed.

I'm Glad I Met You

By the summer of 2004, I'd pretty much given up on the show. Most of the callers were cranks, and taking abuse on live television can drain the life out of you, even if you're doing it with the hope of getting some action. I was probably down to about one non-psychotic viewer, and as luck would have it, she called in. She said her name was Jessica. We had so much fun talking that we stayed on the phone after the show was off the air.

We kept talking off the air over the next few weeks. I had no idea what she looked like, but she was funny and smart so I guess I didn't care.

We finally met each other, and I was stunned at how pretty she was. And how well we got along. I invited her to see one of my live shows.

The event was a literary reading I called "A Tribute to Judy Blume." I know that sounds weird, but here's the context: literary readings in New York City are for people who want to laugh but who fear comedy clubs. You get a bunch of funny, talented writers to read short, funny stories they've written, usually around a wacky theme—à la "Judy Blume"—and unlike at a comedy club, the audience won't get hassled by the performers.

Now, for once, the gods blessed my show and it was a big success. It even led me to becoming friends with Judy Blume, but that's another story. The point here is that Jessica was in the audience. Jessica, with whom I'd been laughing and talking and going out for a few weeks.

Fast-forward a few days. I came home to find a surprise at my doorstep: a bouquet of balloons and flowers and a note that read, "Congratulations! You were great! Love, Jessica."

Now I'd been living in New York for seven years. And I knew, intellectually, that there is nothing cornier than balloons and/or flowers. Particularly balloons like the ones she'd sent me, the ones with the silvery stuff on the one side and the word *Yay!* on the other.

I also believed that relationships are a kind of chess match. Each person tries to conceal his or her feelings of affection in the hope of not appearing desperate. The greatest mistake you could make—at least in my demented way of seeing things—was to let your guard down and make an irony-free show of emotion for the other person.

But the balloons and the note didn't make me feel contempt for her, or that I'd somehow gotten the upper hand. My reaction was something very old-fashioned and corny: I felt . . . *happy*. There was something so genuine and sweet about her putting herself out there like that. With a tiny love note. And balloons. Balloons!

Reflections

That night I sat up in bed. I'd put the balloons and flowers in my room because I was afraid my roommate would see them and laugh at me. The streetlight was reflecting off the silvery stuff, and I was having this chain reaction of emotions and thoughts. I knew Jessica was pretty. . . . I knew we had a great chemistry together . . . but now, now I realized: this was a really good girl! The kind who would be there for me! The kind who was more than just another Manhattan pretty face who'd quickly turn on me. In an instant—and every guy reading this who's fallen in love knows what I'm talking about—I knew she was someone I could get really serious with.

Was it her looks that did it? She's beautiful, but I don't think so. I mean, how many of you have felt a physical spark with someone, only to find out after a few weeks that this person is so bereft of anything you remotely value—kindness, ambition, an IQ—that you know it can't possibly go any further?

What was really making me see her in a new light was the same thing that had made all those guys I'd interviewed see *their* girlfriends in a new light. By her doing something sweet, I recognized she was a decent, generous, affectionate person. And in spite of all the hip-hop videos, in spite of the success of *Maxim* magazine, deep down, guys want decent, generous, affectionate women.

A few weeks later I asked her to be my girlfriend. We've even made the greatest commitment a New York couple can make: we moved in together and signed a joint lease on a Manhattan apartment. I've adopted her dog, Lucy, and I know Jessica and I will be together for a very long time.

Which brings me back to **Why I Wrote This Book**.

A Mission of Optimism and Hope

I wrote it because I wanted to share the basic lesson I learned courtesy of the balloons and the note. To repeat, *What makes a guy view a girl as marriage or serious girlfriend material is her character.* I've made this point to female friends of mine, and almost none of them believe it. They've been conditioned to think that the only thing guys care about is looks, and that we hate even the idea of commitment.

A Question

But ask yourself this. Doesn't just about every guy, at some point between the ages of twenty and forty-five, look for a great girl to settle down with? Forget the Census figures I already cited. Think about your friends and acquaintances. Isn't it usually the guy who proposes marriage? And isn't it the guy who usually wants to go steady, often earlier in the relationship than the girl even wants to? And given that, aren't most of them taking those steps because they sense there's something special about her, something beyond how she wears her hair?

Ask a random guy why he's with his girlfriend or why he married his wife, and unless he's Dave Navarro, he will not say "She aroused me, but besides that, no reason." More likely, he'll mumble something about her being hot AND being "a great person." And it might sound like the "great person" line is a throwaway designed to make him sound less shallow.

It isn't. It's his way of saying he loves her for who she is.

Of course there is a hardcore group of men who will always, ALWAYS be looking for nothing but a short fling, despite the fact that their creepy presence in singles' bars makes people under thirty feel sorry for them. **This book isn't about those guys.** Nor is it about prison inmates, men over fifty with motorcycles, strip club managers, or members of the G Unit.

It's about the other 90 percent of the male population. The regular guys, the ones who become fathers and husbands and make their girlfriends and wives happy. It's about what makes these guys think of a girl not as someone to have fun with for a few weeks, but as someone he wants to keep in his life forever.

Now, the remarkable thing is that what makes men agree that a particular girl is terrific is pretty simple. The key is understanding male human nature. What am I talking about? Read on. . . .

A DISCLAIMER

Perhaps you are wondering what formal qualifications I have to pontificate so freely about love and sex. The answer is that I have no qualifications.

Unlike some self-proclaimed relationship experts, I did not spend literally tens of minutes completing the coursework at a mail-order university.

I'm just a regular guy who likes to give his female friends and his readers the male perspective on whatever they happen to ask me about.

So don't think of this book as a doctor-patient conversation. It's more like a Jerry-Elaine conversation.

Imagine I'm Jerry Seinfeld—minus the millions of dollars and the tendency to tuck button-down shirts into my jeans—and you're my friend Elaine. We're sitting on the couch. There's a bottle of wine in front of us, and I'm going to tell you everything I know about guys and relationships, and maybe even make you laugh along the way.

You should feel comfortable and confident about what you hear, because it really is the frank advice of friends that gets us through life as much as it is the paid advice of professionals.

Also, I can make you the following promises:

1. There will be none of those phony-baloney, relationship-book anecdotes that feature people with generic names like "Janet" and "Steve."
2. You will not be assigned quizzes or crossword puzzles.
3. At no time will the phrase "stone cold superfox" be used.
4. I will assume you are smart and have a sense of humor, as evidenced by the (hopefully) funny, topical "Short Takes" inserted between chapters.
5. I will not try to sell you workshops, seminars, T-shirts, vitamins, sex toys, or ideas I don't personally believe.

If it turns out that you're really bothered by anything you read here, or even if you're pleased by it, don't keep it to yourself. Send an email to greg@doctorgreg.tv, and I'll do my best to respond within forty-eight hours.

And since we're friends, the response is always free.

Don't Torment His Jealous Mind

Not long ago I received a desperate phone call from my friend Sophia.

"The Astronaut is furious," she said. The Astronaut is her boyfriend. He's a graduate student in astronomy, hence the not-quite-appropriate nickname.

"Why?" I asked. "Did you make him listen to your Neil Diamond CDs?"

Sophia is a New York hipster to the core, but has a soft spot for "I Am . . . I Said."

"No," she said. "It's the Bukowski story. He knows it's you!"

A few years ago Sophia wrote a story for a now-defunct

website about why a girl should never date a boy who likes the writer Charles Bukowski. Her point was that guys who like Bukowski tend to emulate Bukowski's beer-drinking, ass-grabbing lifestyle. As an example, she cited a brief fling with a guy who seemed to be dating several women at once when he wasn't falling over drunk. That person was me.

"Now he gets mad whenever I say your name!" she continued. "I told him you're not even attracted to me anymore but that made him madder. I told him it was *three years ago*, that *you* dumped *me*, and that even that was a mere technicality because *I* was too lazy to dump *you*. But he's *still* mad and I feel like I can't even call you when he's around! What's going on?"

It's a good question.

One would think that the success of the women's movement and the popularity of the Indigo Girls would have rendered certain male possessive tendencies obsolete, particularly among those committed to the study of the hard sciences. They haven't.

When it comes to jealousy, notions of equality and politically correct rock 'n' roll don't mean diddly. The Astronaut was pissed to find out that his girlfriend used to sleep with a guy she's still friends with, pissed at the idea she has a male friend in the first place, and just generally pissed in the way guys get pissed when thoughts of their girlfriends with other men flash in their minds.

This chapter is about why you shouldn't exploit that weakness. And why we'll love you more if you make us feel like our natural state of paranoia and insecurity is unnecessary.

But first a little background.

Every girl reading this has dealt with a guy who has gone bonkers with jealousy. She has occasionally been frightened by it and she has probably asked herself this question: why are men this way?

Blame Evolution

One theory is that jealousy has a basis in evolution.

The argument is that the only way our prehistoric ancestors could ensure that the children they thought were their offspring were *in fact* their offspring was to keep a watchful eye on their mates. There weren't condoms or birth control pills back then, so sex meant babies. That meant that if your female mate was having sex with one of your pals, chances are the result would be a new family member.

Jealousy results in behavior that deters our mates from being emotionally or sexually involved with a potential rival.

Now, even if there were, at some point in prehistory, men who had no genetic predisposition toward giving a damn about who their mates had sex with, they'd be eliminated from the gene pool pretty quickly because their mates could very easily be making babies with other men. Wouldn't you be just a little more inclined to fool around if you raised the issue and your boyfriend said, "Go ahead, girl. And tell him I said hi!"

Even more interesting—at least to my inner science nerd—is that some psychologists say that what makes men most jealous today is what their prehistoric ancestors had to worry about most back in the day. Studies show that although women have more anxiety about their men *falling in love* with other women, guys worry more about their women *getting naked and having down and dirty sex* with other men.

Why? Because a sex-charged liaison is the most likely way for a man to realize his worst nightmare: a family of kids that aren't his, and the end of his genetic line. And women? Natural selection favored those who were especially attentive to *emotional* cheating.

This is because if your man falls in love with another woman, he will use his resources to take care of her. After all, a man is more likely to do for a woman he loves rather than a woman he's having a brief affair with. And in the never-ending camping trip that was life before the wheel, "no resources" meant "no food." That meant the end of you and your kids.

Perhaps this is why you see women on *Maury* forgiving men for quick flings, but men going batshit when they find out their girlfriends slept, even once, with other guys.

Studies show that often a woman will forgive her husband having an isolated one-night stand if she believes he still loves her. A man, however, will be driven to insanity if he appears on *Maury* with the woman he loves, and he hears of her sexual infidelity via the words "You are NOT the father!" It's sad to say, but daytime talk shows illustrate how little our sexual impulses have changed since the days when a fire was considered a miracle.

The Jealous Present

Anyway. Even if you think this is bad science, the more important point is that guys are insanely jealous creatures. Whether that's rooted in our biology or our environment is irrelevant. It's who we are.

This means you have power. You can harm us. You can do it in obvious ways, such as by playing an X-rated DVD and saying, "Now THAT'S a cock!" as we sit in the corner whimpering. Or you can subtly erode our self-worth by hinting that other guys are more successful and attractive.

My friend Amanda is a master of this. There's a guy we went to high school with named Christian McBride. He's a jazz bassist. He's won a Grammy, toured with Sting, made tons of money, and is generally the toast of the New York jazz world.

Now every time Amanda's dating a guy, she just HAP-PENS to mention that Chris is touring Japan, Chris is hanging out with Paul McCartney, Chris is the greatest man who ever lived.

You can see the look of irritation on her boyfriend's face when she talks to him like this. It's not a rage that will make him dump her on the spot, but a slowly burning anger that makes him feel bad about himself and, ultimately—even though she'd disagree with me about this—despise the girl who's subjecting him to this nonsense.[2]

So let me reiterate.

Guys are just like you.

Once we're past the initial dance of getting to know you, once we've become exclusive with you, we don't want our waking hours ruined by your taking advantage of our natural propensity toward jealous paranoia.

We want love. Security. We want you to ourselves.

So if you love your man, be considerate. Avoid going on and on about other guys. Think twice about revealing details of your sexual history. And remember: although jealousy is usually seen as a kind of insecurity, it's also a form of desire. A desire to see you with us and only us, to be the loyal girl we envision settling down with. It's what every guy

---

2. FYI, Amanda insisted I keep this in the book and name her by name.

on earth wants now, and it's what they've wanted since the appearance of the thumb.

So don't fight male nature. Instead, apply the words of Judge Reinhold from the film *Fast Times at Ridgemont High*: Learn it. Know it. Live it.

I understand a little jealousy is normal, but my boyfriend is a f##king psycho. He's always calling me at work and calling my cell phone to see if I'm cheating on him. I love him but I can't take it anymore! Help me, Dr. Phil, I mean Greg!

If he's THAT insecure and jealous, then you need to ask yourself whether it's good for either of you to stay together. His insecurity and paranoia might be stemming from the fact that you actually like him a lot less than he likes you, and he's desperately trying to make sure you don't fall into the arms of a superior guy. This problem might be an opportunity to explore whether it's time to let him go.

Now. If I may be brutally honest for a moment, I've noticed that when guys are going into the genuine, certifiable crazy zone with jealousy, it's often when they're in a relationship with a girl who's way out of their league. The moment they feel the best thing in their lousy lives slipping away, the horror of it all makes them nuts. These are the guys you read about in the newspaper who do horrible things.

Other guys are simply insane. They kill people. And they precede their killing by engaging in the kind of behavior you described.

Resolve this sooner rather than later. "Resolve" can mean discussing it openly, letting him know you love him, and moving forward together. Or it can mean a breakup and a restraining order.

Anything else?

Yes.

Some ladies love the drama. The ups, the downs, the arguments, the make-up sex. I've been in a relationship or two like this and they're good for a few months but THEY NEVER LAST. They're like a car riding on fumes. On Highway 1 near Malibu. Toward a cliff. With a laser-guided nuclear weapon closing in on it.

So if you're actually *enjoying* his obsession and torment, and most of your relationship consists of breaking up and reuniting, suspicion and intrigue, consider how far removed from the world of decent relationships you have flown. It might be time to end it. For both of you.

My boyfriend keeps asking if he has the biggest cock I've ever seen. He doesn't. So I lie. But then I feel guilty. Advice?

Keep lying.

But first, let's acknowledge that guys should not ask questions to which they do not want to know the answers. I, for example, never asked girls if I was the most successful performer they'd dated; I knew they'd say no if they'd ever slept with a balloon sculptor.

Because the truth is that compliments on the order of "You're the best in bed," or "Your manhood is so vast, its shadow covers me like those giant flying saucers in the television-movie *V*," tend to be given without solicitation.

Particularly when it comes to the penis. I find those remarks tend to come early and often (the compliments, that is), and if you haven't heard one by month three, you shouldn't ask.

But if he's stupid enough to ask, why not say yes? After all, we lie all the time to protect people's feelings, don't we? Parents, siblings, coworkers, friends: just think of the mountains of benign BS we've heaped on all of them.

So just extend, so to speak, that principal to your very, *very* naïve boyfriend.

What if your boyfriend keeps ASKING about your exes? I mean asking like he's making a file on each one or something.

Look at it as an opportunity.

An opportunity to selectively describe you ex-boyfriends in a way that is favorable to your current one.

Because BELIEVE ME, very few men want to hear about how wonderful any of your old boyfriends were. We don't even want to get the sense that there were *too many* of them. In other words, we don't want to hear about the quality (unless they were awful), and we sure as hell don't want to hear about the quantity (unless there have been fewer than five of them).

I once read that a woman should treat questions about her past lovers the way she would think about filling out a Customs form after returning from a trip to France. You don't want to *lie*, of course, but is it the end of the world if you don't declare every last item?

Here's my problem. My boyfriend is jealous of my friends. My female friends. I've known them a lot longer than I've known him, so it's not like I'm going to abandon them. How can I make him chill out about this?

There are two ways to answer this.

The first is the PC answer you'll find in the women's magazines. Relationships are built on trust, he should have total faith in you, it's up to him to relinquish his insecurities and desire to control you, never give up a good friend for a guy, etc., etc.

And all that is true.

But there's another side to this.

When successful couples start getting serious, friends and family become secondary. There are secrets you as a couple share. Horrendous details about how you really are that no one else knows. Things you get to know about each other that you pray your girlfriend isn't blabbing to someone she probably won't be friends with in a year anyway.

A guy wants to feel like he's number one. This doesn't mean you abandon your friends. It does mean that if they occupy center stage, it is time for them to shuffle off stage left.

What any guy wants to avoid—and again, we're assuming he's not psychotic, just normal-guy jealous—is having intermediary figures in the relationship who will undermine his standing with you. We all have friends who do this to us. No matter how great the person we're dating is, that friend (or family member) will naysay the relationship. Those comments tend to stay in our minds, even if we think we don't believe them.

There's also the question of cheating. Your boyfriend doesn't want your single friends putting you in a situation where you will be tempted to cheat. Nothing unreasonable about that, is there?

Here's the bottom line.

Hold the moral high ground. If you have female friends to whom you don't dish all his secrets, who don't say horrible things about him, who don't encourage you to cheat on him, and with whom you might actually be friends for more than a few months, tell him it's important for you to get out and see your friends every now and then.

If he's an introverted person, he probably won't be totally understanding, but that's too bad. I'm a firm believer that if a person isn't doing anything shady, they project an aura of honesty. So go out with those friends, have fun. And maybe, for the hell of it, pick up your cell phone, call him, and say you're thinking about him and you can't wait to get home. It sounds corny but it works.

I sometimes think my boyfriend is jealous of my career. He's always making fun of my job and rolls his eyes whenever I talk about work. FYI, he's a destitute writer and I'm a manager at an accounting firm.

I deal with this topic more in the "Success" and "Feminism" chapters, but yes, guys do get jealous of their girlfriends' careers when said girlfriends are more successful. That jealousy can be as intense as sexual jealousy.

And let's be frank. The jealousy is not without basis. Most women would, ideally, like to date someone who makes *as much* or *more* than they do. And most men would like a woman who makes *as much* or *less* than they do. When a woman makes significantly more—and there are few disparities greater than the one between a broke artist and a person who has an actual job—it's a Thing. Like an age difference or an ethnic or a religious difference. It's a Thing that needs to be managed.

But just so you know the deal, here's the guy's point of view on this.

In his weaker moments, he thinks of himself as a failure. He thinks YOU think he's a failure. He knows that in a corporate environment, you are going to encounter industrious, economically superior men. No matter that you find them boring or you wouldn't be with him. He feels that on some primal level he's failed you.

His festering resentment about this will occasionally burst through the surface and he'll make comments. He'll ridicule your job. He'll make remarks about the futility of the working life. He'll joke about your having an affair with a coworker. Anything to knock you down a few pegs and bring you down to his level.

I realize this sounds bleak and horrible. But I'm telling you that this is what goes through the dark corners of a guy's mind when he's in this position. Not that I know from personal experience (ahem). Put it this way: it's comparable to how you'd feel if you were forty and so-so looking and he were twenty-five, incredibly handsome, and worked with younger women. There's nothing to *necessarily* make you feel tormented every moment of the day, but wouldn't your mind sometimes run wild with evil fantasies?

But the point here is to give advice, so here's what I suggest.

I'm waiting . . .

Take two approaches. Let's call them sugar and spice.

Spice means don't let all those comments go by without challenge. We all have to let our boyfriends or girlfriends occasionally land a zinger. Not everything needs to become World War III. But it *is* out of line to put you down for something you've worked hard to achieve, something you value or you wouldn't have put so much time into it. When the nasty comments begin, tell him that they hurt your feelings, and could he please not say those things.

Avoid voicing any amateur psychoanalysis about how he's mad only because your success mirrors his failure. That will only crush his spirit and make him wonder if it's possible for the two of you to ever be together given your contempt of him.

Sugar complements spice. Sugar is sweet.

Sugar is telling him how much you love him. How you love and value that he's an artist (or a teacher, or a butterfly collector, etc.). How boring all those corporate guys are.

How it's sexy that he's taken a risk with his life, to live his passion rather than pimp his labor to the man.

There might be an element of benign exaggeration in your sugar, but it is in the service of a just cause: making your man feel loved and valued. There's nothing wasted in that effort. Love and compliments and kind words tend to make their way back to the person who gives them.

10 THINGS
THE MEN OF AMERICA
HOPE YOU WILL REMEMBER

1. Jealousy is the hidden scourge of relationships. Men hate feeling it but they can't help it.

2. Men will not admit when they are jealous.

3. It's up to you to understand what causes male jealousy and to do what you can to prevent it.

4. It's no sin to compliment your man's anatomy, even if you're not convinced that compliment is deserved.

5. Beware of psychos. They kill people.

6. Men can be just as jealous and insecure about your success as they can about rival lovers. In fact, the two jealousies are usually related.

7. There's really no point in going on and on about famous men or celebrities, or the mansion you wished you lived in, or the Ferrari you wished you owned.

8. If your relationship is fueled by the passion of jealousy, you're screwed.

9. Christian McBride is a famous bassist.

10. If your boyfriend is jealous of your career, turn the situation around with the sugar/spice method.

SHORT TAKE #1

Avoid Any Sex Tip Ever Published in a Women's Magazine

Whenever I want to confirm my suspicion that the chances of men and women understanding each other are about as likely as George W. Bush getting booked on *Def Poetry Jam*, I open a women's magazine and read one of those "sex tips" articles.

Are any of these tips capable of causing anything remotely resembling sexual pleasure for a man? I doubt it. Let's go over a few actual items from a recent issue of *Cosmopolitan* to see what I mean.

TURN ON EVERY LIGHT IN THE HOUSE. Great. We stare at my pasty white body while running up the electric bill. I get turned on just thinking of it.

LET'S WRESTLE. What kind of Greco-Roman homoerotic bullshit is this? What's the next tip? Play the soundtrack to *Mamma Mia!* while we watch E! together?

HOLD MY BALLS THE WAY YOU'D HOLD A LITTLE BIRD. I can just imagine my girlfriend trying this one.

"What are you doing?" I'd ask.

"I'm holding your balls like a little bird!" she'd scream. "The magazine said I should!"

"What magazine?" I'd say. "*Field and Stream*? And why are all the lights on?"

LICK BETWEEN MY TOES. This tip is great in theory, but what exactly is proper etiquette when they want to kiss you afterward, and you know it's going to taste like Lamisil?

PLEASURE YOURSELF WITH MY COCK. Is there a guy on Earth who'd prefer this to actual sex? Or a woman who'd prefer it to using that friend of hers in the bedside drawer, the one that looks like a rabbit and uses enough D batteries to power the Space Shuttle?

THREE WORDS: *EDIBLE MASSAGE OIL*. Three more words: leave me alone.

MOVE MY COCK ALL AROUND LIKE AN OLD-SCHOOL ATARI JOYSTICK—UP, DOWN, SIDE TO SIDE, IN A CIRCLE. And am I supposed to make sounds like Frogger? Or jerk my head around as if operated by remote control? And when is she supposed to stop? When I scream "Game Over"?

OFFER UP SOME DIRTY DETAILS ABOUT YOUR EXPERIMENTAL PHASE IN COLLEGE, LIKE WHEN YOU KISSED THAT HOT CHICK. Or how about the time you banged 50 Cent? Or when you serviced two guys in the bathroom of a frat house? Now that's what a guy wants to hear!

SNEAK UP BEHIND ME WHILE I'M COOKING AND UNBUTTON MY PANTS. Because you know what I need when I'm cooking? That's right: some hot canola oil to accidentally singe my joystick.

SQUEEZE AND RELEASE YOUR PELVIC MUSCLES WHEN I'M INSIDE YOU LIKE WE'RE PLAYING A GAME OF TUG-OF-WAR. Yes, it'll be just like summer camp, only in your vagina! Afterward we can wrestle. While I cook. And remember: don't forget those toes.

Don't Destroy Him When You Fight

New York City is cold in the winter.

The wind whips down the avenues, the mayor issues advisories, newscasters solemnly warn of a "severe weather hazard," and anyone who can afford to stays inside. It takes a real idiot to wander those streets without a hat and gloves, but that's exactly what I was doing on a recent night. I had only my jacket, my toothbrush, and my cell phone, and I was determined to roam until . . . well, I wasn't sure until when.

I was in the midst of an epic battle with Jessica, and it had started with a disagreement over Olympic ice dancing.

I'd come home that evening around 9 p.m. My wrists

were sore from a long and not too successful day of writing, and all I wanted to do was kick back and watch people fall in the couples' competition of the 2006 Winter Olympics. I know guys aren't supposed to like couples' figure skating, but I can't help it; I'm a fan. My mother always loved it, and some of my happiest memories from childhood are of her and me watching Torvill and Dean trounce the Soviets. (Freudians in the audience, please discuss.)

So I turned on the TV, pressed pause—we have digital cable—and the image I happened to freeze on was of a woman with her legs spread and her red skater-panties exposed under a tiny skirt. Just then Jessica walked out of the bathroom.

"So you want to look up girls' skirts tonight?" she said.

I can't tell you how much this pissed me off. Something told me this was a personal challenge to my right to have dominion over the remote control, and as nutty as it sounds now (even to me as I write this), I became *furious*. I knew I was violating a cardinal rule of living with someone, which is that . . . if she wants to fight over something insane—such as my alleged attraction to Armenian ice dancers—it's better to let her have her say than it is to initiate global thermonuclear warfare. But hell hath no fury like a guy who thinks his pride is at stake.

And so, for reasons that won't possibly sound normal now—a false accusation about me and a figure skater, the question of who controls the television—I grabbed my coat, put my toothbrush in my pocket, and mumbled something like "I hope you don't think this is just theater because it isn't," and walked out on her.

It took about three steps for regret to set in. But I felt like I couldn't back down, so I just started walking. And walking.

And walking.

My feet were frozen and my ears were about to fall off, but I believed the loss of limb was preferable to a loss of respect. So I kept going.

And there you have what's wrong with men in a nutshell.

We're Morons

When it comes to fighting, we have the reputation of being more fierce, more abusive, and tougher. But the truth is different. When you eliminate the extreme ends of the bell curve—the guys who are abusive and the guys who are indifferent to conflict—you're left with a huge number of men for whom conflict causes them to . . . shut down.

Think about it. We all know a guy who is dating or married to a woman who constantly nags and harangues him. And most times, that guy is not Ike Turner. He's a bureaucrat in a Dostoevsky novel.

He doesn't go into battle over every challenge. He doesn't

live for the drama of the fight and the reconciliation. He's the opposite. He's withdrawn. He's stoical. He'd rather say nothing than provoke another confrontation.

Temper, Temper

Looking back, I think I walked out the door because I felt so angry that I knew I couldn't make a decent argument and win. My rage frightened me. I felt out of control. And it's not that I'm a tough guy. If I were to get a tattoo, it wouldn't be the one that bad-boy literary fraud James Frey got, "FTBITTTD" (F#ck the Bullsh#t It's Time to Throw Down). It would be more like "EMSYSOMTAIS" (Excuse Me Sir You're Standing on My Toe and I'm Scared).

The point is that even in the most mild-mannered gent there is a hair-trigger temper. It sends adrenaline through his veins and gets his heart pumping when there's trouble. That's the reason men rank "low conflict" so high in surveys when asked what's important in a marriage. It's also why a man appreciates it so much when he's with a girl who isn't constantly putting him in "fight or flight-out-the-door-and-into-the-wintry-abyss" mode. In fact, when two male friends get together, and one is reporting that he has met a girl he really likes, he will often begin by saying, "She's so relaxed and nice. . . ."

But more on that in a moment.

Let's first look at what some scientists say is the reason men tend to get so worked up in the face of conflict.

The explanation begins with life fifty thousand years ago.

The Evolution of Rage

Imagine two cavemen.

They are not the hairy, grunting morons you see played by nonunion actors on the Discovery Channel. They are just like men today, only they are foragers on a sparse planet where the average age of death is thirty-two. That's what life was like for early humans.

Now let's suppose that one of those two guys is a sensitive type. He doesn't snap into a violent rage at the most minor slight. He's calm and thoughtful. Always in control. He is John Gray, PhD.

The other is Mike Tyson. When someone gives him too much eye contact, he gets that crazy, Robert Deniro in *Taxi Driver*–look on his face and says, "You looking at me? Because I'm the only one standing here. . . ."

Now. What do you think happens when Mike Tyson and Dr. John Gray come into conflict? In an era when even a minor injury meant death, the more volatile man is the one likely to attack the peaceful one, and hence be around to mate with a female and pass his genes on to the next generation. The sudden rush of anger that men feel in conflict, in other words, put men at an advantage in the competition for survival in that long-gone world. And like our love of food rich in sugar, salt, and fat, and our desire to have sex with the attractive or the powerful, it persists today.

We Are So Very Primitive

Times have changed, but our DNA hasn't.

Men are still more likely to do something impetuous and irresponsible when provoked. Just watch your local news to see what I mean. No matter where you live, within fifty miles of you, there was an event over the weekend deserving a headline like, "Man Shoots Other Man for Giving Him Disrespectful Look."

This is not to say every guy is a killer or that we are unable to restrain some of our natural impulses. The biologically determined craving for sugar, salt, and fat I mentioned earlier doesn't result in most of us being unable to stop stuffing our fat faces with M&Ms and pizza. Men are capable of coping with a rush of emotions whose power unnerves them—and they do it by shutting down and wondering how they got into this mess.

Girls Are Better

Women are different. You have a higher tolerance for the relationship give-and-take. You don't mind exploring emotions or confessing flaws. Not every discussion is a call to war.

Think of the possibilities. If the female way of doing things supplanted the male way of doing things, there'd be fewer murders and fewer wars. There'd also be less professional wrestling, and the makers of Grand Theft Auto would be out of business, but that's another story.

The point is that you're better than we are. We know that.

But with your superiority comes responsibility.

Keeping the Peace

The blunt truth is that your boyfriend doesn't read books like this. He doesn't own the *Mars and Venus Book of Days*, and he probably will not be watching *Dr. Phil* later today. "Relationship improvement" is not on his to-do list, though he may love you very deeply and never want to be without you.

That brings us to the bottom line.

The supposedly tough gender is just as vulnerable as you are when there's a fight. Men become inarticulate and withdrawn when things heat up. And that withdrawal can cascade into a whole set of problems. The chief among these is that two things women cherish—affection and communication—begin to wither.

Despite what all the pop therapists have told you about taking every single opportunity to express and emote and analyze and debate every single negative feeling that happens to pass through your consciousness, realize a man's principal response is to feel attacked, or to detach from the problem and try to solve it quickly and rationally.

He can manage this reaction, but if you think first about whether an issue really merits what amounts to him as a fight (even if it feels like a discussion to you), then *perhaps it's not crucial to bring it up at all.*

So I guess what I'm saying when I say *Don't Destroy Him When You Fight* is more than the obvious comment that when you're, say, arguing over whether he should have bought new paper towels, it's best not to accuse him of being a loser. I'm saying that the very standard of what constitutes "fighting" is so much lower for men, and they place so much importance on there being peace between you, that I really mean *Don't Destroy Both of You by Driving Him Away with Fight after Fight.*

There's a reason guys hold the phrase "low maintenance" in such high regard. It's because where there's calm there's love, and where there's love there's as good a chance for happiness as there possibly is. And that's hard to argue with, wouldn't you say?

I feel like you want women to just be quiet and act all 1951-ish.

Not at all.

Every therapist on earth will tell you that conflict is as ordinary as breathing and that fights can be a means of relieving tension and solving problems.

I'd further add that I used to be in one of those relationships where we never fought. We didn't argue, we didn't experience jealousy, and you know what? *We also never had sex.* We were twenty-six years old AND HAD SEX ONLY ONCE A MONTH.

So while no one advocates a drama-filled, break-up-once-a-week-so-you-can-enjoy-the-make-up-sex relationship, I think a totally conflict-free relationship means (1) one or both of you is too timid to assert your needs, (2) it's passionless, or (3) you're perfect and I want to kill you.

Just thought I'd mention that.

Now as for turning back the clock . . .

I'd like to give a somewhat roundabout answer, while first acknowledging that I'd offer *Of course not! Men want to be challenged! They want a woman who speaks her mind! Who calls him on his bullsh#t! Who's tough and strong and expresses her feelings and tells him he's a jerk if that's what she thinks!*

What the hell are you talking about?

Hear me out.

Several years ago, a psychologist named E. Mavis Heatherington from the University of Virginia studied fourteen hundred couples over a thirty-year period. She wanted to know, among other things, what types of marriages fail and which succeed.

She said the most successful fall into two types. I call them the Blue State Ideal and the Red State Ideal.

The Blue State Ideal features two bright, educated people with professional jobs who share the common goals of a nice house, status in the community, career accomplishment, and, I'd assume, SAT prep classes for their kids that begin when they are still in the womb.

The Red State Ideal is the traditional marriage of the male breadwinner and the female homemaker. This type actually results in the fewest divorces.

Now. One type is modern, one is traditional. So much for the idea that all things need to be as they were in 1951.

But you know what's fatal to each of these? *Too much conflict.* Two-thirds of divorces are initiated by women, but of the one-third initiated by men, the number one cause is *too much conflict.*

Continue.

In 2003, a group of psychologists from the University of Texas at Austin published a study called "The Precarious Couple Effect: Verbally Inhibited Men + Critical, Disinhibited Women = Bad Chemistry." Their argument is the same one I made earlier, albeit with charts and graphs.

They point out that even though one "of our culture's most cherished ideas is that when it comes to communication in relationships, more is better," for many men, "relentless talking may be aversive, particularly if it is critical in nature."

Translation: don't doom your relationship by failing to balance the need to talk everything out with the reality that most men would rather skip the debate and have their day-in, day-out commitment to you speak for itself.

Speaking of red states and blue states, I'm a Republican and my boyfriend is one of those liberals who's always shoving his point of view in your face. Ideas?

A couple can certainly deal with having different political views. Just look at the bald Cajun who worked for Clinton and his wife, What's-Her-Name. What's more important is having a shared *relationship philosophy*, i.e., what you think roles should be, whether you share long-term goals, and whether there's the kind of day-to-day exchange of good-will that gets you through rough moments, such as when

Hillary becomes president and you decide to move to Minsk.

But seriously.

There are all sorts of things about which Jessica and I are deeply and fundamentally at odds, but we somehow get through it.

Take recycling. I am personally unable to recycle, which I realize just made most of you hate me. I really try to separate our trash into the twenty-eight trash cans we use, but invariably I end up putting a soda can where the water bottles should go, or something like that.

I used to justify my lack of coordination by saying that recycling is a sham and that all those separate cans of trash are poured into one giant hole in Staten Island. That just made her want to commit ecoterrorism against me.

My solution to all this is to avoid these subjects. I don't bring up Staten Island and she doesn't point out that I'm destroying the rain forest. These issues are simply not integral to our happiness, just as whether this party or that wins a midterm national election isn't integral to yours.

The dark cloud on the horizon is how the two of you want to indoctrinate your kids. It's a less important issue than what religion they'll be, but I think a kid wants to know what his family stands for. That way, he knows how to find its opposite and drive you nuts when he's a teenager.

I keep trying to get my boyfriend to open up about how he feels about me and our relationship and he just gets this look on his face like he's constipated or something. What should I do?

First, understand that what writer Gertrude Stein once said about Oakland sometimes applies to men and their feelings: there's no "there" there. It's not that guys are without emotions. It's just that sometimes we're being probed about how we feel and there just aren't that many words that come into our heads.

Also, if a guy is dating you exclusively, and he lives with you or is married to you, no matter how fortunate he might be to have you in his life, there is a part of his brain that assures him that if he were single, he'd be having the love life of Kid Rock or Ron Jeremy.

He's not going to *act* on this nagging sense that he could be among the female masses spreading his seed, but he *will* have the sense that *just being with you says enough.* In other words, for him, it is totally unnecessary to say "I love you" every ten minutes because if he's doing his duty as a good boyfriend or husband, he thinks that says it a million times louder.

Here's the irony.

A deadbeat guy will often be more superficially attentive. Especially if you live together, and you're working and he's either unemployed or barely employed, he will try to even things out by telling you all the things he knows you want to hear. Some guys have made an art of this. Don't buy it.

On the other hand, a reminder to your guy every now and then that it would mean so much to you to hear him express his love to you, and *that it doesn't have to be poetic or perfect*, is the best way to approach him.

Deep down I think I'm a guy. My boyfriend is the one always trying to get me to open up and I'm the one who's ready to walk out when there's an argument. How can I learn to be more open?

First of all, people who break up in the heat of an argument *almost always regret it*. A bona fide breakup is usually the result of a long period of disengagement resulting from many, MANY grievances. You get past the point where you want to resolve anything, and you mentally put yourself into the next phase of your life.

And then you dump the person and you both become miserable for exactly 50 percent of how long the relationship lasted.

Second, if you have that hair-trigger, guy reaction, then I have to heed the message men have had screamed at them by pop psychologist after pop psychologist: *just listen*. Don't try to problem-solve. Don't feel attacked. It's part of his process to let those feelings flow. His venting is just a means of unwinding and getting close to you.

Also, you can do what I do.

Ask questions. Don't engage in a debate. Make him express his argument over and over until it is clear that he is two steps from being a mental patient. And once he is in that vulnerable place, suggest having sex.

And this brings us to . . .

10 THINGS
THE MEN OF AMERICA
HOPE YOU WILL REMEMBER

1. Just about the most important thing to men, besides sexual fidelity, is being in a low-conflict relationship.

2. Fighting leads to male emotional withdrawal.

3. That emotional withdrawal is a sign the relationship is in serious trouble.

4. One way to prevent it is to make avoiding fights a priority.

5. I nearly froze to death rather than deal with my petty anger.

6. I guess you could say I am at times pathetic.

7. A little fighting now and then is normal if not healthy and good for the relationship.

8. Men have a lower threshold for what they define as antagonism, nagging, arguing, etc.

9. Most men are not very good fighters.

10. Love can overcome disagreements about politics and recycling.

SHORT TAKE #2

Sex and the City
Is Not Reality

There comes a time in every guy's life, particularly if he is a New York–based dating columnist, when he must sit down and watch a few episodes of *Sex and the City*. That's how I spent a recent afternoon: watching the adventures of four attractive New York women (as opposed to my usual fare, which includes shows that should be called *A Group of Morons Discusses Sports* or *Watch This Family of Idiots Build a Motorcycle*).

My conclusion? The show is smart and funny, but unrealistic. Here's what I mean.

THE SHOW: Samantha Jones, a middle-aged publicist, dates a stunningly attractive young male model.

THE REALITY: Young male models don't date older women—they date other young male models.

THE SHOW: Four women meet regularly for lunch and enjoy years of mostly conflict-free love and friendship.

THE REALITY: No woman in New York has maintained the exact group of friends for more than ninety days. No one with a job has the time to meet for lunch, and nothing will make you lose friends quicker than endlessly bitching about your love life.

THE SHOW: Miranda Hobbes, a successful Manhattan attorney, falls in love with a bartender.

THE REALITY: Successful attorneys don't go to bars, they don't move, they don't bear children, and they rarely engage in the activity they hear described as "dating." They pretty much do the following: make giant stacks of paper in their offices, read said giant stacks of paper, get abused for not reading said stacks quickly enough, and wonder, vaguely, how they can rob a bank to pay off their student loans and make a new life in Tahiti.

THE SHOW: Samantha performs a certain sexual act on a UPS-type deliveryman she just met—and relishes every moment.

THE REALITY: A woman giving sexual favors to a mailman she just met isn't doing it for "excitement"—she's doing it for crack.

THE SHOW: Carrie Bradshaw, a sex and dating columnist, lives in a giant Upper East Side apartment and is known throughout the city.

THE REALITY: I, a sex and dating columnist, live in an apartment the size of a public toilet; write for *Metro*, a free newspaper; and thus am known only to people too cheap to buy the *Post*.

But despite these differences, the show is still one of the best-written sitcoms ever aired. It made millions for Time Warner, and the actresses hated each other. What could be more real than that?

Make Him Feel Like a Success

. . . Even If Deep Down You're Not So Sure

My friend Anthony is a handsome guy with a good heart.

He is also a New York actor, which means he spends nearly every moment of every day wondering whether he should have gone to business school. He works at his father's bread company from seven in the morning till four in the afternoon, where he dreams of having his art pay for his life, rather than his ability to process mass orders of harvest wheat. His life is basically a Billy Joel song, all the way down to the fact that several years ago he met a girl he fell in love with, a girl he would eventually decide to marry.

That was before everything fell apart.

The trouble started a year in. His girlfriend's name was Samantha, and at the time she was also an actress. Now unlike Anthony, who grew up in middle-class Queens, New York, Samantha grew up in Greenwich, Connecticut. And her parents are loaded. Not "her father drives a Benz and they have a big house" loaded, but loaded as in "perhaps her father, if whimsy so directs him, will start a hedge fund this weekend."

Anthony couldn't see it coming, but women who've grown up with that kind of privilege often look for men to duplicate what their fathers gave them. Which is whatever the hell they want, minus the demands of an actual adult relationship.

Can you guess where this is heading? Anthony and Samantha laughed together, went places together, shared acting war-stories together, and, I assume, had a good time in the sack together. I figured they were going to end up married and so did all their other friends. But far away from all of us, Anthony was quietly realizing that in some profound, elemental way, he didn't measure up to Samantha's definition of a success. And that, for a guy, is fatal. Fatal to his self-esteem and fatal to his love for the person he thinks doesn't value him. Let's let Anthony explain:

This is a very simple story but it sort of says a lot. She'd had a tough night at work. And we were in a cab coming back to my apartment. And I was trying to comfort her. And she said, "Sometimes I wish I would have gotten married and stayed in Greenwich and I'd have a Range Rover right now and two kids and I wouldn't have to be dealing with this shit."

I knew that "this shit" didn't mean me—she meant what she'd had to deal with that night. But it was hurtful in a way because I knew that that's the world that she belonged in and it was a world that I couldn't provide for her. And I remember saying, "Well, don't you understand that that's kind of hurtful to me? That, you know—it means I wouldn't be in your life if that was the case?" She never got it. She never got it.

Every guy's been in a situation like this. With me it happened with pretty much every woman I dated before I turned twenty-nine. Because I couldn't point to any sort of tangible accomplishment—such as holding down a job that didn't involve people saying to me "Oh, are you the temp?"— I felt ten times as awful about myself as my girlfriends did about me.

This was compounded by the Boyz II Men Factor. You might remember Boyz II Men. They're an R&B singing group known for their elegant harmonies, their argyle socks, and the many millions of albums they sold during the first Bush administration.

I went to high school with the members of Boyz II Men. And that means that however bad I might have been feeling about my life after high school—taking six years to graduate college, knocking around New York as an obscure play-wright/comedian—my depression was exacerbated by the knowledge that four guys from my high school were, at whatever moment I happened to be feeling down, likely sipping champagne and receiving oral sex on a private jet.

This led to all sorts of preposterous moments in my life, many of which occurred while I was working as a customer service representative in a windowless call center in down-town Manhattan. The office had one of those Lite Jazz! sta-tions pumped though ceiling speakers, which means my worst memories of the place have a soundtrack by Kenny G.

One day as I was sitting there wondering how I'd fallen so far from my glory days at Philadelphia's High School for Creative and Performing Arts, I suddenly heard the sounds of my rich and famous chums, Boyz II Men, literally de-scend from above. The song was "End of the Road."

Every guy deals with this kind of stuff. And it weighs heavily on his self-image. Whatever his idea of the pinnacle of success is, one of his old classmates will be further along in reaching it than he is. The writer for the *New Yorker*, the cornerback for the Kansas City Chiefs, the rapper, the rock star, the published poet, the VP on Wall Street: from age twenty-seven forward, a guy's overachieving peers dance around his consciousness like the little devils from the game show *Press Your Luck*.

And because of this raging storm of torment, a guy is hyperattuned to signs that a woman thinks he's a failure. Once a guy sees those signs, he will become either suicidal or disengaged or both.

My own postcollege dating life has been a constant reminder that I cannot possibly be in a serious relationship with someone who harbors dissatisfaction and disappointment with my status and standing in the world. And although for a long time this eliminated most of the female population, that's how it is. Most men, me included, have this involuntary impulse to identify with their careers.

Have you seen the play *Glengarry Glen Ross*? There's a scene in which the character Shelley Levene sums up what men feel. "A man *is* his job," he says. He means it when he says it, and he's a failed real estate salesman!

The point is that even if a guy is a writer for a newspaper that gets distributed free on public transportation (ahem), or he's boxing loaves of bread for his dad, he wants to be with a girl who admires him. I know that sounds silly and juvenile and un-Women's Studies-ish, but it's true.

Academics might tell you beauty is an invention. But that doesn't mean you don't want to be told you're pretty. A guy is constantly told that what he does for a living has nothing to do with who he is as a person. It doesn't matter. Your boyfriend wants to be, in your eyes, the most successful man on earth. And it's so simple to make him feel that way.

But first let's look at this a little more closely.

Men are attracted to beauty, women are attracted to power: that's the belief of evolutionary psychologists, Maureen Dowd, and the creators of beer commercials and romance novels. AND YET, men and women form committed relationships all the time, despite the fact that most people are neither powerful nor glamorous. Why is this?

My friend Miriam once told me that "my friends and I just want boyfriends. We don't care if they're rich and famous because that would make most of us nervous." I believe her. Ask most guys who, in their wildest fantasy, they'd like to be, and they'll imagine someone like Gene Simmons—the reptilian-tongued member of the band KISS who claims to have slept with forty-six hundred groupies. Meanwhile most women, if you asked them who they'd like to marry, would conjure up someone smart, reliable, handsome, and successful: John Cusack with a thriving medical practice.

In other words, an ideal for women exists, but most women aren't paralyzed by it. How else would all the bathroom attendants and relationship-book authors get girlfriends? Even in the dating zoo known as Manhattan, most long-term relationships begin in excitement, not catastrophically lowered expectations.

Which brings me to Jenna Jameson. And by "Jenna Jameson" I don't mean the Botox-injected person born April 9, 1974. I mean the ideal: tiny waist; huge boobs; big smile; roaring sex drive; a living, breathing middle finger to the feminist movement. The common belief is that she is the embodiment of what heterosexual American men between the ages of fourteen and dead really want, and that her mere existence has raised and distorted standards of physical beauty to impossible levels.

But the truth is that men's desire for the Jennas of the world is fleeting and shallow. As I mentioned earlier, the post–World War II generations have been hooking up and dating since we were teenagers. We have a sense of what's actually based on actual dating and sex. The perfect ten is a fiction. But women still worry.

And men worry, too. Not so much about looks, but about success. We worry that like Maureen Dowd, you only want to date Michael Douglas. We wonder whether you'd prefer the Range Rover, the two kids, and a membership at the Woodway Country Club to what we have to offer.

But we're also easily swayed from these worries.

And that brings us to what you can do.

• • •

The first thing is to remind yourself that the male ego is not a raging lion. It's a teenage girl on prom night. It needs flattery. But said flattery will seem authentic only if you follow my suggestions. I hope you'll indulge me and let me skip the Q&A format as I want to get right to the point:

Never Get Serious with a Bum. Not to get all Dr. Laura on you, but if you insist on dating only guys who are over thirty, live at home, and are thinking of going to film school, you have abandoned your right to bitch about him not being vice president of Goldman Sachs.

Manage Your Doubts. Part of being human and being in a relationship is dealing with the periodic suspicion that someone better is waiting in the wings. But take it from me. As someone who was single a long time: there is no one better. The dating pool is full of lunatics, half-wits, and fans of Tucker Carlson. If you've found someone with a good soul who makes you laugh, cling to them like grim death. More than a few women have dumped a sincere, intelligent guy because they wanted someone more handsome and successful. Their fate is ongoing loneliness and an unending membership to Match.com.

Remember That Your Complaining about His Income Is Like His Complaining about Your Looks. It's hard to think of anything more offensive than a man criticizing his girlfriend's looks. And I don't mean how she dresses. I mean her face, her ass, how her legs look in biking shorts. Yet this is how guys feel when their income is attacked. It just seems like it should be off-limits. This doesn't mean avoid all discussions about money. Nor does it mean that people who love each other don't feel tension and argue about finances. It simply means that you should appreciate that you're playing with fire, and that what you say will be hard to forget.

Refrain from Sounding Awed by Other, Richer Men. A few years ago I went to see the movie *Pearl Harbor*. The first close-up of Ben Affleck comes on screen. "Now that's a movie star," my alleged girlfriend says. My reaction? An instant wish for a cinderblock to fall from the ceiling and smite me. For a long time, I couldn't enjoy anything on earth about Mr. Affleck. Not *Good Will Hunting*, not the Red Sox winning the World Series, not even the critical reception to *Gigli*. And it wasn't his looks that worried me, though he does have a strikingly full head of hair. It was the sting of that comment. I'd have felt the same way had she said the same thing about Pauly Shore.

Trumpet Not the Triumphs of Guys His Age. As I suggested above, there is nothing more painful to a guy than the success of his contemporaries. That is why the only friendships that succeed where there is a vast difference in income also have a vast difference in age. So if you're aroused by Jack White and your boyfriend is the same age, *keep it between yourself and your gay friend.*

If You're Glad You're with Him and You Support Him, Say It!
Remember Anthony? I recently ran into him. And he had the relaxed, happy demeanor of a man whose love life is going well. "I'm seeing someone new," he told me. I asked whether she, too, torments him with visions of Range Rovers and picket fences. "A few weeks ago we're walking out of a restaurant and she just stops and tells me how proud she is of what I'm trying to do with the acting and the working and everything," he said. "I feel like I'm myself again."

Now that's success.

SHORT TAKE #3

The Mystery of Lesbian Until Graduation

Even certified dating columnists like me are sometimes late in discovering new dating trends. Until a year ago I thought My-Space was a storage company, and the first time I heard the phrase "rainbow party," I thought it was Ralph Nader's new environmental group. "How can I contribute?" I believe I said.

This brings me to a term some of you, like me, only began hearing recently: Lesbian Until Graduation, or LUG. Apparently our nation's fanciest colleges are bursting with young women who are homosexual for eight semesters, after which they collect their diplomas, kick off their Birkenstocks, and begin searching for jobs and husbands.

LUGs, of course, should not be confused with guys like me

who lived with their parents during college. We are known as CUGs, or Celibate Until Graduation.

GIRLS GONE WILD

Social conservatives would have you believe two things about the LUG phenomenon. The first is that it proves people can be "cured" of being gay, since it seems all it takes is a degree and a bus ride back home to set tens of thousands of young women straight every spring. The second is that it illustrates the general moral decline of young America.

I don't buy either argument. But you have to admit things are different than they used to be. Maybe it's *Sex and the City*, maybe it's what happens when kids grow up listening to 2 Live Crew. But girls today are without a doubt wilder than they used to be.

I'm not just talking about collegiate lesbianism. I mean the provocative photos that college students post of themselves on Facebook.com. I mean those *Oprah* segments you see about teenage girls doling out oral sex like free bobbleheads at a Mets game.

And don't get me started on teachers. In my day an English teacher looked like an English teacher. She was old, angry, and the only thing that excited her was the proper use of the subjunctive. Today your high school English teacher not only looks like Jenna Jameson but acts like her, too.

THE REAL WORLD

But how much of this is bad news? If experimentation in college has gone from having outlandish political ideas to having outlandish political ideas and, for some women, a same-sex partner, who's being harmed?

Remember: life at the top colleges is like camp plus hormones and alcohol. You get four years in which to walk around barefoot, invent political controversies to become outraged about, and sleep around.

Then you hit the real world, and for many of us, it's "Girls and Guys Gone Mild."

Be Nice to His Mom

... Even If She's the Devil

So I used to date this older woman.

She wasn't old compared to, say, the cast of *60 Minutes*, but she *was* twice my age: I was nineteen, she was thirty-eight.

It was the summer of 1992, and I was still living in my parents' house. One day I was home alone, probably listening to *Dark Side of the Moon* and wondering why I wasn't organized enough to go away for college, when the doorbell rang. Standing on the porch was the woman my friends would later call Queen Krazy.

She was around five feet tall, had on a short black cotton dress, and, with her thick black frames, looked like a forty-year-old version of Lisa Loeb, which I realize is a strange description, since Lisa Loeb now looks like a forty-year-old version of Lisa Loeb.

"I used to live in this house," she said. "It was in the seventies. I've always wanted to see it again."

I let her in. We walked around the house. And maybe it was the short dress, maybe it was the sultry, contaminated Philadelphia-in-August air, but somehow I knew that very soon this woman and I would be naked together.

After the tour we exchanged phone numbers. I bicycled to her house for a visit about a week later, and before you could say "MILF," I was entangled in a passionate romance with a woman born five months before Bill Haley recorded "Rock Around the Clock."

Strange Days

Now besides our age difference, Queen Krazy was not a normal girlfriend. I probably should have had a clue she was slightly off when she told me about an episode at a used comic book store called Green Onions.

"I asked the guy behind the counter if I could use the bathroom, and he was all like, 'That's for employees only,'" she said. "So I was like, 'Okay,' and I peed right there on his fucking floor. Why are you staring at me?"

Now I, being at a point of low self-esteem familiar to

young men with no future living in crappy cities, stayed with her because, like a Meredith Baxter-Birney character in a Lifetime movie, I felt I could do no better.

This is slightly off the point, but it's a little-discussed fact that many men are in bad relationships because of low self-esteem. Our girlfriends make us miserable, but we figure sticking with them is better than subjecting ourselves to certain rejection in the dating marketplace. We'd all feel a great sense of relief if we could share our sadness with someone, but besides our being unable to afford therapy, gender expectations are such that if a guy confesses that he is with his girlfriend because he thinks of himself as a loser, the person listening to him will also think of him as a loser.

But back to the story.

A Not-So-Wise Decision

Queen Krazy and I continued to date for a few months. And it was always a horror show going out with her—she'd fight with waitresses, try to sneak into movies without paying, run into old boyfriends and argue with them on the street, and generally be a nightmare everywhere but the sack, which is the deal you make with Satan when you date a woman who's Krazy.

So. Given that I was involved with someone for whom a

genuine personal improvement was that she wouldn't relieve herself while perusing used books, I did what any decent guy would do.

I introduced her to my mother.

Shock and Awe

The apocalypse happened at a house my parents had just bought in Bucks County, Pennsylvania. Queen Krazy and I drove there in a 1978 Buick she had stolen from a disabled acquaintance of hers (long story). Being a completely whipped, beaten-down shell of a man, I spent the entire trip worrying about whether Queen Krazy would approve of my mother and stepfather.

It now seems a bit silly that my priority was to see to it that the woman who had given birth to me, nursed me through illnesses, worked her ass off to send me to private school for a few years, and even pretended not to be aware of the copies of *Penthouse* in my closet would be sufficiently deferential to whomever I happened to be dating. But such was the man I was in those days.

We sat down to dinner. And I don't remember too much about what happened next except that the conversation consisted mainly of Queen Krazy holding forth about why my parents were evil for not supporting the Sandinista revolutionaries in Nicaragua, as well as why she will always be pro-choice, given that she'd had not one but THREE abortions. She also suggested that I drop out of college so that she and I could hit the road and attend the Telluride Film Festival that fall.

The reaction of my parents was stunned silence.

It was then that I had a simple thought: *Gee, it would be nice to be with someone my parents don't hate.*

The Big Picture

In fact, as I've made the shift that almost all guys make, from wanting to sleep with every girl alive, to wanting to be with one wonderful girl I can sleep with every night, and laugh with, and share my work with, and sometimes just be around and do nothing with, the more I've come to appreciate girlfriend–parent harmony.

And this all goes back to what I've been saying about character and values.

History

I once read that in the 1950s, the Miss America pageant didn't crown the hottest girl, the best violinist, or the girl with the best plan to eradicate diphtheria. Back then, Miss America was the girl you'd want to bring home to Mom, or whom your mom would most like you to bring home. And that meant she was more the sweet, smart girl from college than the stripper-type every guy's been having erotic fantasies about since he was eleven.

I think, actually, that there's been a paradoxical harkening back for men to the old-fashioned notion of a girl who makes Mom happy. We live in a time when even nerds start having sex at fifteen, and they can easily have short-term flings well into their forties. Given that sex is so available, the incentive to marry just to get laid is gone, which means that if you're going to marry someone, she damn well better have more qualities than being good in bed.

And there's something else.

Reality

You often hear that most of a relationship is spent NOT having sex. And that's true, especially in my case. When you're going really steady with someone (a phrase that sounds so much more fun than "getting serious" with someone), you're fusing two lives. And it really is a colossal pain in the ass when there are conflicts between your parents and your girlfriend. And it really is such a relief when they get along. It even makes going home for holidays okay. It even makes you think, *Wow, this family-oriented, nonsex part of the relationship isn't that bad.*

So think of yourself as a diplomat when meeting his mom. The man in your life will be so grateful if you're successful.

Now. Life is rarely a simple matter of having niceness solve all problems, so let's get to the questions.

It's been more than a year since we've been dating and my boyfriend hasn't introduced me to his parents. Another book would probably say He's Just Not That Into Me. What should I think?

I think women today need to be ever aware of whether they've become a Booty Call Plus. A BCP is a girl you're sleeping with, you go on dates with, you're maybe even exclusive with, but in your heart you know it's not going anywhere. Only you're either too much of a wimp to end it, or you're selfishly waiting till someone better shows up. More than a few of us have been on either end of that situation.

Now, a guy will not introduce a BCP to his parents because he knows she won't be around much longer. So yes, something is amiss if a year's worth of holidays has gone by and you haven't met his mom, especially if he's met yours.

On the other hand, there might be a perfectly innocuous explanation. Maybe he's in a phase in which he can't stand his parents. Maybe he's afraid they'll offend you. Maybe he's met your family, thinks they're fantastic, and prefers spending holidays with *them*! Come to think of it, isn't there usually one member of a couple whose family is more dominant?

The only way to know is to ask. If you're not the kind of person who's good at talking about uncomfortable things in person, send him an email. (I know that sounds ridiculous if you live together, but a short email, perhaps sent from work, can spare you an awkward conversation.) It may be that his parents have told him that they only want to meet a girl he's planning to marry, in which case bringing this up will get you information on quite a few things you might have been wondering about.

I have a different problem. My boyfriend introduced me to his parents a month into the relationship. It freaked me out since I'm not sure I want to get serious with him.

Ah, the errors guys make. Here's his likely rationale: since the longer you wait to make a parental introduction, the more the tension builds, he was probably thinking he could diffuse the situation by having them meet you early. *That doesn't work.* Like getting her name emblazoned on your right butt cheek, introducing a girl to your parents is a sign of commitment, and should not be done before you're certain you'll be together for a while.

My advice? Let it go. Chances are that it was a tactical mistake, not a sign of abject desperation.

I hate to say it, but I haven't brought my boyfriend home because my family is blue collar, and I'm worried our velvet paintings of Elvis and my father's rifle collection are going to freak him out.

The standard answer here is to say you are who you are, be proud, he should accept everything about you, blah blah blah. The truth is that some of us have sprung from humble origins and moved to places like New York City or Los Angeles for the specific purpose of breaking free from small towns and small minds.

My suggestion? Lower his expectations. Make it sound like you grew up in a Frank McCourt memoir. Have that boyfriend thinking your life was so miserable that if he does meet your family, the sight of indoor plumbing will make him rejoice.

And remember this. For every person worried about his or her humble origins, there is an equal and opposite person worried about being a snob. I've been fortunate enough to attend a variety of schools, from the crumbling piles of crap known as Philadelphia public schools to an Ivy League university. Whenever I've been around fancy people, I've noticed that it is extremely easy to make them feel guilty and/or wish they'd had a "real" childhood in a tough city. Little do they know how violent, stupid, and mean the world can be beneath a certain economic line.

Unless you've made the decision to be with a jerk, if

your family background is more modest than your boyfriend's, he will be more than understanding and patient, especially if you have carefully manipulated his expectations and sense of guilt.

I'm African American and my boyfriend is white. I want to get along with his parents, but what the hell am I supposed to do if they're racist? Keep my mouth shut if they use the "N" word? I don't think so!

Good point, and I have a few thoughts on this. But first, isn't it sometimes a pain in the ass to be part of an interracial couple? I say this as someone whose high school girlfriend was African American. Beyond the issue of introducing your beloved to your parents, you have to deal with all the normal stresses of a relationship, in addition to which you have to listen to every idiot's political/sexual/perhaps-even-racist interpretation of your love life, sometimes yelled at you while walking down the street.

Of course this can also build an intimacy and sense of togetherness otherwise hard to come by.

Anyway, I was blessed with very open-minded parents—see above—but plenty of white guys weren't. And so I think it's up to your boyfriend to be firm and clear before he introduces you that (1) he loves you, (2) you might be in his life for a very long time, and (3) certain comments are out of bounds.

Another thought: have the first meeting in a public place where the two of you are not the focus. A play or a wedding, for example. That way everyone is in a good mood, looks their best, and is maybe even acting their best.

Finally—and this is totally un-PC, so get your keyboard ready to write me a letter—turn down your sensitivity meter a few notches. Many people still make politically incorrect remarks in their own homes regardless of race, age, or background. You, Reader, irrespective of the fact that you might listen daily to NPR, might occasionally make a politically incorrect remark in your own home.

So if your man's parents say something truly awful, call them on it. You're under no obligation to tolerate a racist environment. But chances are, if your boyfriend has made his wishes clear before you met, they won't be screaming epithets from a bullhorn while you pull into the driveway. You'll just have to deal with the normal family nonsense: weird food, awkward conversations, and the sudden desire to run home screaming and sleep in your own bed.

What if we want to get married? The last thing I want is a riot on my wedding day!

A wedding is your day, not theirs. An acquaintance of mine and his African American girlfriend recently decided that both of their families could kiss their asses, flew to Greece, and got married there. It was just the two of them.

When they returned, they had separate social events to celebrate with each family.

Was that solution something out of a 1950s sitcom? No. Is life ever a 1950s sitcom? No.

You talk about different races but what about different religions? My parents are Evangelical Christians and my boyfriend is Jewish. Suggestions?

Well, the stuff above about interracial couples applies, but there's a special temptation a nice Christian girl dating a Jewish boy must avoid: lying early to her parents about his religion. Remember: marriages can begin with what you think will be a short fling. So if you're the type who chats with her parents about whom she's dating, don't tell them you're dating a Christian if he's Jewish. I learned this from an acquaintance that is indeed an Evangelical Christian and is now married to a Jewish guy.

She was upfront early with her bible-thumping parents. They saw the relationship evolve, and the news of their getting married wasn't as much of a shock. So even though they believe her husband is eternally damned to the fiery flames of hell, at least they smile when they see him.

A few other thoughts on this. We live in a time in which you can find just about any sort of minister or Rabbi to perform whatever kind of ceremony you can dream up. Besides churches, synagogues, and mosques, there are mountaintops, chapels, beaches at sunset, and roadside motels in which to conduct nuptials. So don't think that the relationship is doomed because you won't be able to have a traditional or religious wedding.

We're going to his place for Christmas this year. I have the whole week off and so does he. How long should we stay? The idea is to leave before we kill each other.

Three days, maximum.

And I don't know about you, but I find that if I don't plan family activities, my mother sits me down in the living room and stares at me while waiting for me to say something witty. Because I am completely exhausted by the time the holidays arrive, and every particle of my DNA seeks nothing but rest, I end up staring back blankly and annoying her.

So toss in a movie or a dinner at a restaurant. It'll spice things up and take the pressure off you. Then you can spend your time attending to normal holiday anxieties, such as whether your family will figure out how little you spent on their gifts.

10 THINGS
THE MEN OF AMERICA
HOPE YOU WILL REMEMBER

1. Don't do anything psycho in a used comic book store.

2. Fear not if we introduce you to our parents sooner than you think is appropriate.

3. Confront us if you feel we're hiding you from our families. The first meeting should occur before the relationship is one year old.

4. If you're worried the first meeting with our parents will go badly, schedule that meeting for a public place in which all are required to dress nicely.

5. Any concern you feel about our reactions to your crazy family can be mitigated by overstating how crazy your family in fact is.

6. If you fear a catastrophic meeting because you are of a different race, creed, or ethnicity than your man, make said man do the necessary prep work to keep his parents in check. Also . . .

7. Don't get too worked up about tiny remarks that are un-PC. Not everyone has the sensibility of a first-year Wesleyan student.

8. Keep visits under three days if you're staying in the same house. It decreases the chances of fights.

9. Schedule activities. Too much sitting around the house breeds conflict.

10. Be nice to our mothers. Really nice. *It will make us love you more.*

SHORT TAKE #4

Wanted: Internet Profiles That Don't Suck

Some people never learn. Internet dating has been around more than a decade, but online profiles are still as rife with lies and clichés as they are with bad photos. Here are the phrases that top my list of ones that need to go.

"I'M REUBENESQUE." I'm not sure which "Reuben" is behind "Reubenesque," but judging from appearances, it's either Ruben Studdard or the guy who created the sandwich. But the truth is that lots of guys love big girls, so there's no need for the fancy talk. Tell it like it is: "Large Booty-esque."

"LOOKING FOR A PARTNER IN CRIME." What are we going to do, sell crack together? Dress up like we're in a dinner theater production of *Clue*?

"I AM A GENEROUS GENTLEMAN." Any guy who uses this phrase should just write "I Am an Aged Chump Looking for a Prostitute."

"OLD-FASHIONED GIRL." How old-fashioned are we talking here? Old enough that you want to be huntin' varmints while I pan for gold, frontier-style? Because if you mean "We won't be getting naked till there's a ring," just say so.

"CRAVING A MAN WITH A SENSE OF HUMOR." Yeah right. I've been a funny guy since I was eight but girls didn't give a crap about my jokes till I got a decent haircut and an apartment that didn't have a shared bathroom in the hallway. What women *really* mean is "craving a guy who satisfies all my criteria concerning looks, age, and income, but additionally makes me laugh, but in a witty not clownish manner, unless of course he is filthy rich, in which case I'd get busy with Carrot Top."

"SEEKING A CASUAL RELATIONSHIP." Translation: "Seeking a Prescription for Valtrex."

"LET'S EXPLORE THE CITY." Why? Why do so many women want to explore the city? Is there a treasure buried under a public toilet? A river that needs charting? Why not keep it simple. Suggest doing what normal couples do. We can watch TV, argue, and, when we're alone, scan the personal ads for a good laugh.

Stop Worrying About Feminism

I **wasn't going to bring this up.**

After all, this *is* a dating advice book. It should have quizzes and puzzles, perhaps a cartoon of two people kissing on the cover. Maybe even the number 7, 10, 100, 101, 1,000, or 1,001 in the title, as in *1,001 Reasons She's the One!* Anything but politics. It's not like you'll ever catch John Gray, PhD, weighing in on the deficit. Dr. Phil, when he's not berating people on his TV show, doesn't hold forth about Iran's nuclear plans. So why am I bothering with something as volatile as the "F" word?

Because lately I've been noticing something. It has to do with the aforementioned "F" word, and it concerns every smart woman I know who's between the ages of twenty-five and forty-five.

They're worried.

Not about the usual stuff: appearance, career, and how to find a decent straight guy who also happens to have a pulse. I mean they're worried about the whole ball of wax. The view from fifty thousand feet, as business school grads would say. They are concerned that what Maureen Dowd suggests is true: that the more a woman has accomplished professionally, the less attractive to a man she becomes.

Through Dowd's articles in the *New York Times*, and thanks to female übersuccesses like Martha Stewart having less-than-electrifying love lives, it's become conventional wisdom in some quarters that women might do well to turn the clock back to the 1950s. Not many people are saying it outright, but that's the inference: if success drives men away, then women should abandon all this man-repulsing work stuff, and return their focus to whether Junior has eaten enough vegetables or whether the windows are clean.

This chapter is about why that particular view is bullshit. It is about why guys *want* a woman with a career. But before getting into that, let's go over a little history.

History

The American woman has been raised on the idea that she can have a fulfilling life only if she has a career. She read *The Feminine Mystique* in college; she took back the night. Even if she hasn't, she has divined this message from a million other sources: there's more to life than washing dishes and waxing floors, and that "more" is having an education and getting a high-powered job.

It wasn't always this way. Notions of the sexes being equal are relatively new. Putting aside the thousands of years of outright, unambiguous oppression, it wasn't until 1964 that men even knew about the clitoris. Sex generally lasted thirty seconds and was followed by a demand for a steak. All women were referred to as "gals," including heads of state, nuns, and grandparents. The *New York Times*—and here I'm being serious—had a separate category for "Women's Jobs" *until 1971.* You can imagine how many of those ads were for attorney, surgeon, or police officer.

Things began to change in the 1970s. Title IX, which prohibits discrimination in education, was passed by Congress in 1972. Roe vs. Wade legalized abortion in 1973. Billy Jean King beat Bobby Riggs in a "Battle of the Sexes" tennis match also in 1973, and in 1980 the Go-Go's released

91

"We Got the Beat." I realize this is a horrendous summary of the women's movement, but the point is that in classrooms and in corporations, barriers to women's advancement were officially dismantled, and all the while young women were on the Pill, and guys read *The Joy of Sex* and learned how to give good oral. I call that progress.

Today

It is now perfectly normal for teenage girls, when they're not hypnotized by too many hours on MySpace or deafening themselves with their iPods, to envision careers in law, medicine, business, government, or science. Many adult women have those careers. I've dated some of them. They were born in the early 1970s, went to fantastic schools, and although they thought I was a complete loser, they were not averse to a serious relationship, or even balancing the demands of work, love, and even parenthood. What worried them was how I and my gender feel about all this female empowerment.

The message I bring is this: stop worrying.

But hasn't feminism screwed with guys' heads, either by making them think they should be wimpy and Art Garfunkel-ish, or by causing a backlash and driving them to listen to Rush Limbaugh?

Any guy born after 1970 has had the virtues of equality, diversity, harassment policies, speech codes, Take Back the Night, and Tori Amos preached to him since birth. There are militia members, fundamentalists, and Wahhabists who haven't, but if you're reading this book, I doubt these guys are on the top of your to-date list.

Most guys my age have absolutely no problem with what mainstream feminism stands for. *The word itself* makes our collective balls shrivel. But that's because we associate it with the lunatic fringe that believes all intercourse is rape, and heterosexuality has been socially constructed by evil males in order to oppress women.

But don't most women object to those crackpot theories as much as we do? A 2005 CBS News national survey found that only 24 percent of women consider themselves to be feminists. I think this shows the radioactivity of the word, especially when you consider that probably 80 percent agree with the central principals of mainstream feminism—equality in education and work, and legalized abortion. Most men, by that definition, agree with mainstream feminism.

Guys under age forty have been working with and for women since they entered the labor force. All this chatter about men not feeling like they can be men, or of their feeling intimidated because women work, is nonsense. And remember this tidbit: guys my age were teenagers during the Clarence Thomas hearings. And based on that viewing experience, I can promise you that not many of us plan on asking our coworkers about Long Dong Silver, whether they enjoy pubic hairs in their soft drinks, or any other overtly harassing behavior.

Any other thoughts, as clearly this has caused you to rant?

Yes. Most guys are more than a little aware that leading a remotely middle-class life these days requires two incomes. We have also been brought up to think that a wife or serious girlfriend is a person you actually talk to. Now besides consigning you to a life of poverty, having only one partner work seriously limits conversational material. This sounds trivial, but I've spoken to guys who feel quite dismayed to come home from work and find a partner whose contribution to the evening's dialogue is "The baby pooped."

I still think it's a problem when a woman makes much, much more money than the guy does.

You're right. In the interest of keepin' it real, let's acknowledge an uncomfortable truth: women don't like marrying way, way down, and men don't like dating way, way up. But

I still think relationship conflicts rarely boil down to only this, or that income disparities necessarily doom relationships.

I know a successful woman attorney. Her husband is a doctoral candidate in physics at NYU. She makes many, many more dollars than he does. But she feels like they're equals because she appreciates his intellect and ambition. He knows that like all corporate lawyers, her job makes her miserable, so his mild envy of her income is mitigated by knowing she's always looking to do something more personally fulfilling, like going back to grad school and getting a PhD.

Do they argue over who gets to pick where they go on vacation? Of course. But are they also a very successful couple that spends more time being happy than not? Absolutely.

What do you think of those most famous of relationship books, Men Are from Mars, Women Are from Venus **and** The Rules? **The authors seem to play into gender stereotypes, but I liked the books.**

The publication of *The Rules* is the single most important publishing event since Guttenberg churned out the Bible. For years, everyone had been buying into the idea that dating problems can be solved only by extensive psychotherapy, and that any sort of strategizing about "getting" a man was beneath the modern, educated woman.

The problem was that the modern, educated woman needed to get laid. She also needed a serious boyfriend or husband, and all the politically correct, Freudian nonsense floating around seemed a lot less useful than the kind of commonsense advice you could get from a friend or a parent. The key points of *The Rules* are that (1) men enjoy a chase, and (2) there's no shame having the acquisition of a husband be a major life goal, a goal that requires patience and thought.

So two ladies from Long Island got together and wrote a book that gave detailed advice on how not to seem desperate. The idea was that by being unavailable for phone calls, dates, and sex, guys would actually like you *more*.

Now, the political left went apeshit when this book came out. How dare they make women play games! Who are they to say a woman should need a husband! Oh, the humanity!

Meanwhile, the book sold a trillion copies and sparked two sequels, and I think they still offer "Rules" telephone therapy sessions on their website for ninety-nine dollars an hour. One of the authors got divorced a few years ago, which pretty much shot their credibility as relationship gurus, but the point and the money had already been made.

But you know what? Those women were right. Being a little unavailable in the early stages of a relationship *is* important, unless of course you really, really need some action.

Men Are from Mars, Women Are from Venus is a similar story. For years, people had been assured by academics that men and women are exactly the same and that it is only modern, capitalist society that makes us different. Meanwhile, common sense told the rest of us that innate differences may be behind why men are more likely to commit murder, start wars, listen to Iron Maiden, look at pornography, attend Monster Truck pulls, nod approvingly at cars that play "La Cucaracha" when you press the horn, and, most important to John Gray, PhD, "go to their caves" when they are upset.

But John Gray, PhD's actual advice is uneven. When it comes to the bedroom, for example, he says, "for sex to be great there must be loving and supportive communication in the relationship." In my experience, dim lighting and cheap alcohol are much more effective.

I also have to wonder about his whole deal. Have you seen his website? He's peddling not only books but also board games, DVDs, seminars, wellness treatments, and "Mars and Venus Super Shakes." What's next? Mars and Venus karaoke CDs? To answer the question, yes, the books play into stereotypes. But they also have lots of useful advice.

Here's something I've been wondering. I read Susan Faludi's Backlash, and she says that there's a crisis of masculinity in America. What do you think about that?

It's bunk.

At some point in 1992, every smart woman writer began

believing a bunch of horseshit about men becoming bewildered and confused and flummoxed and probably impotent thanks to the women's movement.

This confusion supposedly comes to a head when a guy takes a girl to dinner and the check arrives. Maureen Dowd makes a big deal about it in her book *Are Men Necessary?*

The argument goes something like this. As the server plunks the bill on the table, the guy is paralyzed by the questions that ricochet through his mind. *Should I pay? I guess I should, but isn't that sexist? Should she pay? But if she does, aren't I complicit in postfeminist sexism? How about if we both pay? Should I permit her to pretend to pay, then actually pay? Will she think I'm a chump if I let that happen? Wait a minute. . . . Where is she going? Why is this happening to me? WHY GOD WHY????*

Listen.

First of all, it's unlikely that any male today is going to make the mistake of taking a woman to a fancy restaurant on the first date. Every woman has had a miserable first date; if you're wondering why guys avoid Le Cirque on the first date, imagine having to compound that misery by paying $250, not including tip.

Second, and I hope I can make this clear, WE DON'T MIND PAYING. There are deadbeats and money grubbers out there, but overwhelmingly men know that it's their job to pay. That's the premise. We accept it. You accept it. There's no crisis.

Now—and I'm giving insight on the male mind here, so don't hate me if the following is annoying news—there are times in the middle of a date when I have figured out the girl and I have absolutely no shot, either because she has the personality of Teresa Heinz Kerry or because she has some-how communicated that she'd rather get run over by a bus than date me.

At that point, I might just accept her phony female reach for the wallet and let her pay half. But that's because I'm cheap, not because the fact that I've read Susan Brownmiller keeps me from getting a hard-on.

I have a different problem. I think having kids and actu-ally raising them yourself offers a much better way of life than schlepping off to work each day and having your children brought up by someone from an Eastern European republic that no longer exists. I'm worried people will look down on me because this is what I want. Your thoughts?

Let me answer with a story.

Several years ago I was a temp on Wall Street. I'd shuffle onto the subway every morning and sit at a desk from nine to five. I made fifteen dollars an hour. Compared to what everyone else makes on Wall Street, economists will tell you that that hourly rate "ain't shit."

At the time, I was living in SoHo with a female friend.

She was born in Connecticut and had a modest trust fund, which is the law if you're from Connecticut. The fund's monthly payout enabled her to stay home while I was creating Excel spreadsheets for guys five or six years my junior. And even though she wasn't my girlfriend, I'd sit there all day, periodically stewing with envy, wishing I could stay home, too.

But there was this little voice in my head. It reminded me of an uncomfortable truth, which is that a woman who stays home to take care of the house is a "homemaker," while a guy who stays home and tends to the house is a "loser."

I am a man, and my lot in life is to work. If being home is that important, then I need to find an occupation that permits it, such as abetting Nigerian Internet scammers or hosting Amway parties.

So the short answer is that of course it's okay, even admirable, to be a homemaker. But I think you need to make sure your husband or boyfriend feels that way, too. Your decision is probably based on his making enough money to support both of you, so just be sure as you get closer to marriage that both of you are comfortable with his being the sole earner. Some men want that very much. Others are cheapskates—I mean "progressive-minded men"—and want their partners helping to cover that cable bill.

Could you please just level with me and tell me whether deep down men want a quiet girl who's younger and stupider, and who cooks, cleans house, and looks like Sophia Loren in one of those movies where she runs around the desert in a loin cloth?

This is sort of like asking whether deep down women really want a rugged poet with a private jet. One that is as rich as he is romantic, and who will beat someone's ass who threatens you. He is also gentle and loving and a great listener, enjoys apple picking and foliage viewing, and is completely devoted to you.

The answer is that there is probably some part of our fantasy life that wouldn't mind it at all, just as we wouldn't mind finding a bag of money, having wings, or reading a "Shouts and Murmurs" column in the *New Yorker* that actually makes us laugh.

But these are fantasies. They aren't going to happen. And to be honest, none of that kind of fantasizing comes into play when I'm thinking about my love life. I don't even think I'd be happy with someone like that. I'd feel like I was stuck in an episode of *I Dream of Jeannie.*

The point of this chapter is that guys today aren't intimidated by their equals. They're who we usually end up marrying, and we often meet future spouses in the workplace, where we've supposedly been made so screwy by having women there in the first place. It's true that some female billionaires might have trouble finding men who aren't intimidated by them. But basing your view of the dating world on the experiences of billionaires is as foolish as me worrying about Dan Brown's financial problems as I concoct another book proposal.

So keep climbing the corporate ladder. Or drop out for a few years if you wish. You have more options than any women in human history. When it comes to dating, your career, by itself, is nothing to worry about.

10 THINGS
THE MEN OF AMERICA
HOPE YOU WILL REMEMBER

1. We don't mind paying for dinner on the first few dates. You can offer some money just to be nice, and that gesture will not make us go insane.

2. I am the worst historian of the women's movement ever.

3. There are more women writers worrying about whether women should have careers than there are men worrying about whether women should have careers.

4. Please email me at greg@doctorgreg.tv if you've purchased John Gray's Super Shake so that I can find you and smack you.

5. The American male's "crisis of masculinity" is a myth.

6. Being rich can hurt a woman's love life, but most of you are not rich, so get over it.

7. Being a homemaker is nothing to be ashamed of, especially when you consider that the working life means sacrificing most of your waking hours to gossip, meaningless labor, and singing "Happy Birthday" to people you hate.

8. Most guys, even though they'd hate to admit it, are "feminists" in the sense of agreeing with the basic ideas behind mainstream feminism: equality in education and at work, and legalized abortion.

9. Most guys are not averse to having their girlfriends work and be successful, especially when they consider how this state of affairs will diminish their contribution to the monthly mortgage payment.

10. Working girls are sexy.

SHORT TAKE #5

"Date Night"
for the Insane

I hate to pick on *Redbook* magazine, but a recent article of theirs has given me no choice. The headline is "100 Great Date Night Ideas," and while it gives the reader one hundred ideas, the first word that comes to mind when you read them isn't *great*. It's *disturbing*.

Let's go over some of their suggestions to see what I mean.

FIND A BRIDGE AND WALK ACROSS IT; THE VIEW CAN'T BE BEAT.
I don't know where this writer grew up, but I'm from Philadelphia, where finding a bridge and walking across it means finding a crackhead who'll toss you into a river after he robs you for your shoelaces. *¡Que romántico!*

TAKE A TOUR OF THE HOUSE YOU'D (SOMEDAY) LOVE TO OWN.
Sounds great, but I'm not sure Mr. Hefner would let us in.

RENT A FANCY CAR. TOOL AROUND AS IF YOU ACTUALLY OWN IT.
Let me get this straight. I drop $1,000 to rent a Ferrari, pretend I own it, then give it back. The only thing I can imagine more depressing is the look on my girlfriend's face when I hand in the keys.

DRIVE OUT TO A COUNTRY FIELD, LIE DOWN, AND SNUGGLE UNDER THE STARS. Then watch as your beloved is carried away by pitchfork-wielding yahoos.

SAMPLE INTERNATIONAL FOOD AT A STREET FAIR. Have you seen the food they serve at these street fairs? What are we supposed to sample, a botulism sandwich?

GO OUT FOR PIZZA—ASK THEM TO CUT THE PIE INTO THE SHAPE OF A HEART. If I made this idiotic request at the pizza joint I go to, it would no longer be "Date Night." It would be "Watch the Pizza Guys Beat Greg with Giant Wooden Spatulas Night."

ONE WORD: FRISBEE. One more word: never.

ENJOY A ROUSING GAME OF TWISTER. Then enjoy a rousing trip to the emergency room after you dislocate your clavicle.

PICK UP A BUCKET OF FRIED CHICKEN AND HEAD FOR THE DRIVE-IN. What kind of Jerry Springer-esque life do they think I'm living? Should we also get tattoos and join a militia?

HIT A HIKING TRAIL NEAR YOU. This is actually a good idea.

GIVE EACH OTHER HAIRCUTS. Since the two of us aren't barbers, I think we'll stick with going out to dinner and/or renting a movie.

MAKE A TIME CAPSULE ABOUT YOUR DATING DAYS TO OPEN TEN YEARS FROM NOW. In it will be an envelope. Inside will be a message from your lover. And it will read, "No more date nights."

Keep Looking Good

. . . Even If You're Sure He'll Never Dump You

I once knew a girl who was beautiful. Let's call her Tammy. She and I went to graduate school together.

In the fall semester of our first year, Tammy and I were assigned a video project. Now some of you have gone to film school or to journalism school, and you know how stressful producing a video piece is. There are late nights, long road trips with cameras and lights, and endless hours in dark editing rooms. In those rooms you either befriend the person you're working with, or become so frustrated that you can't help plotting how to make his or her death look like an accident. Tammy and I became pals.

Fast-forward one year.

I was sitting in a professor's office when there was a knock on the door. It was Tammy. She hadn't been to the school in months, but she had a very happy look on her face.

"I'm married!" she said, waving a hand attached to an obscenely massive diamond.

We clapped. We hugged. And we let her go on and on as she made it clear that her new husband had tons of bucks and status and all that other stuff guys secretly hope you couldn't care less about.

But as she was talking, I couldn't help noticing something.

Her hair.

It used to be long and straight and lustrous and sexy. Now it was short and bobbed. A year ago she'd looked like a model. Now she looked like a member of a Beatles tribute band.

It made me sad. Sad that I'm a shallow bastard who harps on these things, and sad that something every guy secretly worries about had come to pass before my eyes: that commitment leads to pretty much everything we initially found sexy about our girlfriends slowly disappearing.

Don't Hate Me, I Come in Peace

This might sound contradictory, but guys are actually kinder in their judgments about appearance than you think. We are all happy being with a regular girl. The tragedy is when that regular girl who turns us on so much seems to have stopped caring. We take it personally. We know that you wouldn't be doing it if we were in an early phase of the relationship. That in a sense, we're being punished for making ourselves so available to you.

Women aren't as judgmental about looks—at least not to the same degree. This makes it hard to understand this complaint. It sounds petty and mean-spirited. But I'd be less than honest if I didn't say it was true.

To complicate matters further, we so much appreciate you when you take that extra moment to look pretty. Whether it's putting on makeup, or wearing something besides a sweat-suit twenty-four hours a day (unless of course you're over fifty and live in Florida, in which case it's the law), those small efforts makes us happy. The sad thing is that we rarely express that appreciation. But more on that in a moment.

Courtship vs. Commitment

I'm not the first person to talk about how love leads to becoming hideous. Oprah did a show on it. Howard Stern has talked about it on his radio show. And the men who called in basically had the same observation: that things sexually went into the crapper once their wives cut their hair short. Dr. Laura, who some of you probably find more offensive than Mr. Stern, has a whole section in her book *The Proper Care and Feeding of Husbands* devoted to chastising women for what she calls the "Frump Syndrome."

You can guess what she says. Men are simple. We want sex. The least you can do is look good and keep us happy in the sack. Avoid living in clothes that look like they could also pack Idaho russets. Put on foundation. Etc.

All that is good advice. But I think it's much better to look at the whole issue in terms of how both guys and girls change once we know we're in the I–Doubt-I'm-Going-to-Get-Dumped Zone. Men are particularly horrendous. We gain weight. We go days without shaving. We rerun outfits.

I'm particularly bad about this. I have this light blue Ramones T-shirt I don several times per week. It was in style for about eight minutes in 2002, but I persist in wearing it. I'm sure Jessica has spent many a moment looking at it thinking, *I wanna be sedated.*

Have I forgotten anything? Oh yeah. If you're with us long enough, we lose the hair on our heads and sprout riotous tufts of it from our noses and ears.

Many of us stop making any romantic effort whatsoever. Gifts, going to exciting places, wearing clean underwear—all those things go out the window once we've been dating you for more than 120 days. So not only do we fail on the physical side, we collapse on the emotional one, too.

Then there are the contradictory signals we send you.

Guys might *say* they want a girlfriend who keeps herself looking good, but we can sabotage a woman who's trying to do just that. How many of us will call you at the last minute—in blatant violation of *The Rules*—and invite you out to dinner, only to give you only fifteen minutes to get ready? Or roll our eyes when you're "taking too long" to get all dolled up? Or not appreciate you when you wear something sexy to bed? Or make fun of you for buying new clothes, even though that's supposedly what we want?

There are no innocents in the crime that is the post-courtship collapse.

Frump Nation: An American Crisis

I have to share an observation.

Frumpiness does not plague the rest of the developed world as much as it does America. In my vast travels around the globe—as well as when I watch foreign films on the Independent Film Channel—I can't help noticing that the women of Latin America, Italy, Spain, France, Asia, Eastern Europe, and yes, the Russian Federation, seem to value dressing up and looking feminine much more so than here.

You will never find in Florence or Paris, for example, the sartorial apocalypse you can witness any given afternoon at the Mall of America. Women abroad, especially the ones who are over the age of thirty-five, really do seem to care more about looking good even if—gasp—they're married.

And yes, even the guys dress better. This isn't saying much, as in many parts of this country you can find men going to weddings in those baseball caps that have the moveable wings on them. My point is that even though Frump Nation might be part and parcel of the casualness and friendliness of American culture, I think we can retain our openness while we learn something from our more dapper friends abroad.

Please don't think this is a case of me being a New York metrosexual jerk looking down on the heartland. I look down on you for keeping *Left Behind* on the bestseller list, nothing more.

And by the way, New Yorkers are in no position to judge anyone. There is a neighborhood in Manhattan called the Upper West Side in which you will find haggard-looking zombies stuttering to themselves as they walk down the street with back copies of the *New York Review of Books*, wondering why they can't get a date.

These aren't homeless people—they're writers for the *New York Times* and faculty members at Columbia.

A Plan of Action

The nitty-gritty advice is this. Whatever the hell you did in the first couple of months, keep doing it. If you live in Dallas, keep getting manicures and pedicures, devoting 90 percent of your income to buying new clothes, spraying perfume, going to the gym, and getting your hair done twice daily. If you live in San Francisco or Portland, keep bathing every day.

I know this takes effort. The difficulty will be compounded by the fact that however much your presentation is spiraling downward, your man's will be spiraling twice as fast. Feel free to bring up his disgraceful appearance; we take that kind of criticism far less personally. Treat us like the subnormal animals that we are: give us the task (buying new stuff and eating less), offer a reward (be creative), and we will do it.

And we will be so very happy if you do it, too. Because we love to look at you.

Hey, idiot. I have short hair and both I and my boyfriend are much better looking than you are. Who the hell are you to nag me about this, anyway? I thought this book was about the truly important stuff in a relationship.

This question was asked by a certain female friend of mine, one who's probably reading this right now and looking forward to when she can heckle me at a book reading. I will give the rest of you the answer I gave her back in the winter of 2006.

There is a reason people are willing to believe that a makeover given on a TV talk show can revolutionize a person's life. It's not that properly fitting, expensive jeans will *in fact* make a person's problems evaporate. But we believe it, and we submit to that narrative over and over *because we know appearances count.*

I know some of the folks reading this chapter are annoyed. These may or may not be the same people who watch those talk shows, spend thousands of dollars each year on clothes and makeup, and soak in the beauty and fashion tips in women's magazines, all of which are indirectly harsher on the female psyche than li'l old me.

My goal here is to frame this in terms that the average guy is thinking about.

He's not thinking about why you aren't rail thin.

He doesn't give a damn about full lips or thin lips.

He might wack off to a perfect ten, but that fleeting experience in Fantasyland no more affects his actual life than reading *Us* magazine makes a woman quit her job and go hunting for Brad Pitt.

If you're in a stage where you've both renounced all other lovers and become exclusive, and you've had good sex or better, he might be on his way to loving you and wanting to spend a very long time with you.

Here's my point: **he doesn't want you to lose your looks because of neglect.**

That doesn't mean looks are everything or that there's an impossible ideal to attain. As I mentioned, there is that ideal, but it's perpetuated more by women than by straight men.

Talking about guys and looks just makes me depressed. How am I supposed to impress him when all these women's magazines have pictures of models who are six feet tall and weigh ninety pounds?

Women's magazines reflect the beauty standards of demented New York editors and their gay male coworkers, not the standards of guys you want to date.

Has any straight guy ever put a poster of Kate Moss on

his wall? Of course not. The reason? Guys don't like women who are that tall and skinny. The women in men's magazines are always rounder and more voluptuous than what you'll see in *Vogue*. Same with the girls in porno. (Or so I've heard.) There is even a specific market for guys who like big girls. One of the magazines that caters to it is called *Big Butt*. There is no comparable magazine of fashion models called *Emaciated Ass*.

In fact, since we're talking about beauty, let me put this out there: women are far more worried about weight and body type than men are. The range of weights we find sexy is far, um, *wider* than what most women believe is attractive.

Perhaps there's an analogy to be made between how women feel about body type and how some men feel about their manly regions. Of course both things *matter*, but men can be perfectly delighted by a girl who's on the plus-sized side of the spectrum, and there are many women who are perfectly content with a guy who's on the non–Trident thermonuclear missile side of the spectrum.

What's up with guys wanting these Brazilian bikini waxes? Are you all a bunch of latent child molesters?

The popularity of the Brazilian bikini wax fascinates me. I don't know how many of you know about this grooming style, but it involves a COMPLETE AND TOTAL RE-

MOVAL of all things hirsute south of the belt buckle. For some reason, this state of pubic affairs has been associated with the great nation of Brazil.

And, to add to the strangeness of it all, it seems like in 1997 the only girls who had them also happened to make their living dancing around a pole. Then in 1998, with the speed of a wax strip flying off the collective mons, EVERY girl in her twenties or thirties was as smooth as a . . . as a person who'd been given a Brazilian bikini wax.

Opinions differ on their value. Some women say it makes them feel clean and sexy. Others think it's creepy. If your boyfriend insists you get one, I suggest you tell him you'll do it—but only if he will, too.

When my boyfriend and I first started going out, I'd wear clothes that were pretty revealing. Now that we're together, I'm worried he thinks I'm dressing like a two-dollar whore. What say ye?

Stay sexy.

If he's criticizing you, it's not because he's opposed in principal to how you dress. After all, it's what got you together in the first place. There's probably one or two other issues at work.

It might be that he has a controlling personality, and he puts down how you dress as a way to exercise authority over you. This will only get worse. It begins with forbidding cleavage and ends up with him locking you in the basement. Challenge this nonsense early.

Relationships demand an enormous amount of benign compromising, and there's nothing intrinsically wrong with wearing what pleases your partner—most guys actually enjoy giving up some of the responsibility of what to wear to their girlfriends—but you have to be careful if his wish to cover you is a sign of something worse.

This is a slight digression, but you may have observed that the extent to which a society permits women to dress in sexy outfits correlates with how free women are in those societies in general. In parts of northern Europe and the United States, you can walk around almost naked. In parts of the Middle East, it will get you stoned to death.

So you have to ask yourself, Is my man a social Democrat, or is he in the Taliban?

You said there was another reason. And lay off the political analogies.

Yes. When a guy doesn't want a girl showing what her mama gave her, it may be because he doesn't want her attracting the attention of other guys. In other words, if you're much hotter than he is, the last thing he wants is every person in the world noticing what a ridiculous match the two of you are.

One last possibility: you might in fact be dressing like a complete tramp. I've dated more than one stripper in my life (not at the same time, unfortunately), and while I hate to generalize about a group that's suffered as much oppression as go-go girls, many of them dress like background characters from the movie *Pimps Up, Hoes Down!*

To figure out if your own lack of taste is behind his criticism, employ the Carmella Soprano Criterion. Ask yourself: If Meadow Soprano wore this outfit, what would her mother, Carmella, say? If it's "You are NOT going out in THAT," perhaps your man is on the money.

My boyfriend just moved in with me. And I try to look good for him, but when you live with someone, it's impossible to do that all the time. There are going to be days when you're sick, have a breakout, need to shave places men don't think need shaving, or just need time to stare at yourself in the mirror for a few hours. Your thoughts?

This question leads us to discuss the ignorance of the male sex.

Most guys, even when they're going someplace important, such as a prom or their own wedding, will spend no more time getting ready than it takes to watch an episode of *The Daily Show.* On TIVO. Without the commercials. A shower, a brush of the teeth, a shave, maybe an extra two or three minutes on the hair: we're talking around twenty-two minutes.

Things are more complicated for women. They take more time, and they involve mysterious activities and lotions. We know that whatever it is you do, it works, and that's about it.

Given that, what do you do when you live with a guy? What about those days when you need not only time to beautify, but also to be alone for the sake of just being alone?

Let me help you.

As I write this, Jessica and I live in a Manhattan studio. Now for those of you for whom the word *studio* evokes images of the cavernous SoHo art studios you have seen in films like *Hannah and Her Sisters*, think more of the cell where Clint Eastwood slept in *Escape from Alcatraz*.

It's one room. The "kitchen" is a refrigerator and a stove occupying one of the walls. There are no other rooms. There are also no secrets, no places to hide, and if we want to have a private phone conversation, we must slowly die inside. Given this, how does Jessica handle her inevitable need for privacy?

She throws me out on the street.

Before we moved in together, she told me there would be times when she'd need to be alone. Being selfish, I immediately seized upon this opportunity to let her know that I will be spending most Sundays in the fall watching football, and that her silence will be an essential part of my enjoyment of this experience. It sounded like a good deal to both of us: I spend some evenings in a café; she enjoys a New York Sunday when my unlucky team—the Philadelphia Eagles—is playing on television.

Thus a potential conflict became a means of us both getting what we want.

She gets solitude, and I get to watch overpaid felons try to kill one another. Our home is a modest but happy one.

What about when I'm sick and horrible-looking?

Taking care of a sick girlfriend brings you closer together. Guys *enjoy* taking charge and doing that sort of stuff. If your boyfriend lacks the character to stick by you when you have the flu, you should be looking for another place to live and another person to date.

10 THINGS
THE MEN OF AMERICA
HOPE YOU WILL REMEMBER

1. Men have a far more flexible definition of what is sexy and beautiful than women think we do.

2. We love it when you do those extra things that make you look even prettier: wearing flattering clothes, putting on makeup, etc.

3. Men are bad at expressing this appreciation, but when reminded that we should be offering more compliments, we are happy to oblige.

4. Men are guiltier of post-commitment frumpiness than are women.

5. Men are less likely to take offense if told our appearance is going to hell. Don't be afraid to tell us if we're in a downward visual spiral.

6. Speaking of which, I wear the same T-shirt way too often.

7. Women drool over ultra-skinny fashion models more than men do. Men like the rounder look of a 1950s Playmate far more than the look of a heroin-addicted runway girl.

8. There's nothing wrong with demanding the time you need to look your best.

9. I'm guessing Brazilians would like their nation to be associated more with achievements in art and science than with aggressive pubic grooming.

10. Men take it personally if you let things go physically, but "letting go" doesn't mean normal aging or putting on a few pounds. Guys accept this as part of life, and experience it as much as you do.

SHORT TAKE #6

Why You Will Not Meet a Man in the Supermarket

Somewhere out there is a supermarket that's a singles' paradise. It has a DJ and strobe lights. Celebrities fill its produce aisle. Scantily clad women and überhandsome/successful men peruse its selection of Hot Pockets. A velvet rope keeps out the rabble, and every time you visit, you are likely to go home with someone fantastic or, at the very least, obtain his or her IM handle.

For the rest of us, there are brightly lit warehouselike structures in which the wretchedly dressed look for the cheapest can of tuna. That's the kind of supermarket I go to. It's called Gristides and it's on York Avenue in Manhattan. Were I to approach a woman in it and ask her out, assuming she wasn't old enough to own a Pride Jazzy, she'd probably douse me in pepper spray before fleeing in abject fright.

My point is that meaningful relationships rarely begin in supermarkets. And the underlying idea—that meeting someone is easy and can happen in random locations—just isn't supported by the facts. People meet, overwhelmingly, through friends, through family, at work, at school, and, to a far lesser extent, online.

You'll see in the bonus chapter how to realistically increase your odds. But for now, let's keep the supermarket for what it was made for: irritating us with long lines, inspiring impulse purchases of US Weekly, and making us wish we were someplace with a DJ and strobe lights.

Let's Get It On:
The Sex Chapter

Several years ago I was in the green room of a now-defunct cable talk show about sex and dating called *Naked New York*. Now by the time they'd booked me, the show was clearly on its deathbed. Every sex columnist, porn star, porn director, writer of erotica, and D-list New York media critic had already been on a thousand times. Keep in mind that was in the year 2000, several years into HBO's *Sex and the City*, a time in which there were approximately three hundred sex columnists for every person having sex. They'd been through all those folks, and now there were only people like me, "public access personality Mr. Greg."

But back to the green room. I'm sitting there and next to me is a naked porn star named Erika Kole. My segment isn't starting for another hour, and she's on after me, so that means lots of quality naked time awaits us.

I'm trying to avoid looking at her. Because besides making me blush, I'm worried her nakedness will cause me to walk onto the set with the same reaction below the waist as if I were fourteen again and watching *Porky's*.

So I pick up a magazine. It's my old favorite, *Redbook*. On the cover a headline reads 53 SECRETS TO MAKE SEX SIZZLE. I figure I can always use a new secret, so I turn to the article. "Test your balancing skills by making love in a hammock late at night," it says. "When the neighbors won't be able to see!"

This brings several things to mind. The first is, *Where do these people think I live, Gilligan's Island? I've never even seen a hammock, let alone thought about making babies in one.* The second is the thought I have whenever I read these god-awful "sex tips" columns, as suggested by the Short Take you read earlier.

Women have the wrong idea about guys and sex. They think we want the complex when we crave the same three or four things, done well and with abandon, that you are familiar with if you've read Judy Blume's *Forever* or watched HBO after midnight.

It seems ridiculous to say this, but even though fewer topics are more discussed, more studied, and more read about than sex, I think many women today still have some bad ideas about what men are and what men want.

So here's what I'd like to cover.

1. The differences between men and women when it comes to sex.

2. Why men feel vulnerable in the bedroom and how you can benefit from this.

3. Why sex is both crucial and not so crucial to the success of a relationship.

4. Fun stuff we like in bed.

5. Your questions.

That's a lot of incisive brilliance to impart, so let's turn down the lights, put on that Marvin Gaye CD, and get busy!

Quality Time

Ask yourself a question. How long would you need to know a person before you slept with him? Three months? Three weeks? Three dates? Three minutes, if his name is Brad Pitt?

In his acclaimed book *How the Mind Works*, Harvard

psychologist Steven Pinker discusses a study in which good-looking people were hired to approach members of the opposite sex on a college campus and ask them the following: whether they'd like to (1) go out on a date that night, (2) come over to their apartment that night, or (3) go to bed with them that night.

These are the results:

	Women	Men
Yes to the Date	50%	50%
Yes to Going to Apartment	6%	69%
Yes to Having Sex That Night	0%	75%

Does that mean one out of four guys were decent enough not to go for the sex that night? Not really. Of the 25 percent who declined the sex, "many were apologetic, asking for a rain check or explaining that they couldn't because their fiancée was in town."

I recently conducted my own study to confirm these findings.

I began by asking every woman I know whether she would enjoy having sex with a different successful, sexy, handsome, disease-free, nonmarried, straight guy every week for the next year. It would be somewhere secret, and he'd never tell a soul. They all said no, though of course they all first asked where in New York City one can actually locate a successful, sexy, handsome, disease-free, nonmarried, straight man.

I then asked my single male friends the equivalent. If the offer were on the table, would they sleep with a different beautiful girl once a week for the next year? They all said the same thing. It was some form of "Yes. Yes I would have sex with all those girls. And in fact I have envisioned such a state of affairs every moment of every day since I was thirteen."

Quality vs. Quantity . . . Since the Dawn of Man!

It's hard to argue that men aren't genetically predisposed toward sexual variety, and are in many ways more quickly and powerfully aroused. Anyone who's been in a singles' bar at closing time has noticed this. And of course there's a Darwinian explanation for it.

The key concept is what biologists call "parental investment." It's better known to you and me as "some very obvious facts of life."

Parental investment is a measure of how much time and energy a person commits to his children. For women, it's nine months of having the baby inside you, followed by several years of total dependency outside you, followed by a decade or so of torment combined with near total dependency. It makes sense that the person having to do it would be quite discriminating about who she chooses to mate with.

If given a choice, she would prefer a mate who has the resources and disposition to help her, and to protect her and her children. She wouldn't benefit from multiple lovers, since she could have the same number of kids with one responsible, sexually capable guy. Her most important criterion in a mate, according to this argument, would be *quality*.

So important is this question of quality that throughout the animal kingdom, bevies of females will attach themselves to a group's dominant male. Among elephant seals, 80 percent of a herd's females mate with a single alpha male. They are happy to share if the male is of high enough quality.

Human males want to be that alpha seal.

Reaching a sexual climax takes just a few minutes—or in the case of most guys on prom night, a few seconds. And if you look at sex strictly as a strategy for passing your DNA along to the next generation, seeking the most partners would be the best way to accomplish that. I mean, why stay with one female when you could be impregnating so many others? It's not that genes have motives or intentions, or that prehistoric men had a conscious strategy of fathering more children; it's that evolution favored promiscuous males because they had the most offspring.

And that's the essence of the battle of the sexes, at least when it comes to sexual desire. One wants commitment, the other wants booty. (These are technical terms, I know, but try to follow me.) Darwin called the tension between men competing with each other for as many reproductive opportunities as possible *sexual selection*, and it's part of the foundation of his theory of evolution. No wonder it scares some religious fundamentalists. It's much nicer to think of lust as something planted in our minds by the devil than as something as natural as rivers and trees.

Girls Are Better

Men really are a mess when it comes to sex.

I remember listening to the public radio show *This American Life* a few years ago. The topic was women who are getting sex-change operations to become men. One of the women interviewed had begun taking her testosterone pills when she noticed something strange.

She was at work making photocopies. And she was just standing there doing her thing when . . . BAM! She suddenly became so sexually aroused she almost *started humping the Xerox machine.*

Now. Can you guess what every guy listening to that thought, including the dweeby listeners of public radio? They thought . . . *I know what you mean.*

Not a day has gone by since adolescence that I and every

other male haven't devoted an enormous amount of brain power to thinking about sex. It's really quite appalling. And I DON'T mean while looking at porn (which of course I, as an upstanding citizen, have never seen), going to strip clubs (which I hate even when I have money to burn), or doing research for this chapter. I mean while driving a car or worrying about whether you need a new belt.

Blame our degenerate ancestors. We are the result of people who wanted sex and babies so badly, they risked life and limb for it in the harshest conditions imaginable. It's sad to think that millions of years later we get thrown off our game when the lighting isn't right or the CD starts skipping. Just think of how it was before there was soap, lingerie, or Jack Daniel's.

Silver Lining

There's a silver lining to the dark cloud of gender difference.

The vast majority of guys you think of as marriage or serious boyfriend material, i.e., who have some education, no felony convictions, and a desire to have a family one day, are far more interested in a successful monogamous relationship than they are in living the life of the aforementioned elephant seal.

And Yet We Are Needy

Sex makes us nervous. We feel like the burden of a good encounter is strictly on our shoulders. Oh, we may come up a bit short on the execution. But by and large, we think of little else besides how to make women feel awed by our prowess.

You doubt me? Then think about what makes the average twenty-five-year-old guy or girl insecure. When a woman worries about her bra's cup size, or whether she's fat or her feet are too big, she's worried about how she *looks*. When a guy wants to leap off a bridge because his cock is too small, or when he wants to impale himself on the bedpost because he just came faster than the length of an early Beatles tune, it's because he feels he cannot or has not pleased a woman.

Women place great import on elements of sex men barely notice. One guy I interviewed said his girlfriend would't have sex with him unless she felt pretty. This meant that if it was a Saturday night, and they'd met at a restaurant, and she was dressed in a sexy outfit, his chances for some action were great. If, however, he wanted to bust a move the next morning when she was meandering around the apartment in sweatpants and flip-flops, no dice. I think it's fair to say most men are ready for sex whether they're wearing a Prada suit or a chicken suit.

Getting Specific

Most of us have had great sex, even if we were alone at the time. I won't bore you with trying to define it. But in the many interviews with guys I've conducted for *Cosmo*, I've found that what makes men happy sounds pretty unspectacular: no whips, no chains, no midgets carrying torches while the soundtrack to the *Gipsy Kings* is playing. A surprise blowjob from a girlfriend, the sight of her naked body, her moans of pleasure while he's going down on her: these are the things that make guys happy. Simple. Nasty. The possibilities are infinite.

So let's narrow the focus. Let's talk about what *not* to do. Volumes have been written on how men can screw up in the sack. But there are still many women out there who don't know some basic rules for making their partner happy, i.e. . . .

- **Speak Not of Another Guy's Anatomy.** So you dated a dwarf who was hung like Seabiscuit. The current man in your life doesn't want to know. Even if you wish to ridicule the tininess of an ex-boyfriend, be aware that you will immediately emblazon on your current guy's mind the image of another man humping you.

- **Don't Fake It.** Don't wail if you're the quiet type; don't thrash your head around like Linda Blair in *The Exorcist* if you are not possessed by Satan. And if you experience greater sexual intensity by slowing down, then men of America beg you not to demand we speed up. And for the love of the Almighty, don't fake orgasm! Most guys who are over twenty-six have been having sex for at least ten years. They've had multiple partners and they know the difference between the real and the fake. And there's nothing more discouraging to a guy than being with a girl who's pretending. Not that I know this from experience. But I've been told these things. . . . The point is that if you do engage in orgasmic chicanery, a guy's thoughts will immediately turn to *why*, which will invariably lead him to blame himself.

- **Don't Apologize or Feel Worried about Your Sexy Body.** Let me put this simply. WE WANT TO SEE YOU NAKED. Guys spend billions of dollars to see photos and videos of naked women. We know most of you don't look like Photoshopped porno tarts, but we don't care! We like big asses! We like *you*! And if you're confident about yourself, that's even sexier!

- **Refer Not to a Wanton Past.** Few fates are worse than asking your girlfriend to do something kinky or semi-kinky and having her respond, "I don't do that anymore" or "I used to do that but that was in my ho phase." It makes you think, *Why am I always the jerk who's too late at the party?* Or, *Why don't I have the power to make her act all nasty and lovely?* The answers he'll concoct will put him in need of a Zoloft prescription.

- **Avoid the Handjob.** Unless you work in a massage parlor, the handjob should have no place in your life. I believe it was banned by international treaty in 1961. The reason? Every guy on earth would prefer to go home unfulfilled than endure the pathetic experience of his partner giving him a conciliatory substitute for actual sex. Think of it this way: you can't do it better than he can do it himself.

- **Don't Tease.** Whether it's the third date, the third month, or the wedding night, the right guy will wait till you're ready. But please: no false promises. No putting your mouth near his manhood only to say, "Maybe next year." No getting naked and having him sleep over when you plan to wait till your honeymoon.

This brings me to the most important nuts-and-bolts piece of advice I can offer. Psychologists have studied the frequency of sexual intercourse over time among long-term lovers, and have come up with incredibly complex ways to chart it. Ignore them. According to my research, there are three phases of a couple's sex life:

1. Lots of sex.

2. Some sex.

3. No sex.

The objective is to float somewhere between 1 and 2 for as long as possible. And how to accomplish that? Book after book has been written to give you an answer. Some authors suggest "date night." Some suggest mutual masturbation.

I have another idea.

Lazy Sex

Like I said, you will not read this tip in any other book. It has never appeared in a women's magazine and it is unendorsed by the National Organization for Women. Sex counselors around the globe and even your gay best friend will tell you it's wrong. But I urge you to ignore them because what I am saying is true.

Lazy sex is the key to a good sex life.

Here's what I mean.

There are times when the man you love will be aroused. Times when both of you are tired. Times when the prospect of assembling incense, music by Sade, and anything remotely romantic seem as far away as I am from ever being mentioned in the same breath as Thomas Pynchon.

In those moments you can rebuff your partner because you think sex will be a pain in the ass. Or . . . you can give it that extra second or two. Let him try to turn you on, even though you might both be about to fall asleep. If you let things move forward, gently, but with minimal foreplay, you may find that the resulting sex, which proceeded from sheer laziness, is quite satisfying. And as something you experience periodically, as a complement to the wild and crazy stuff all the books tell you you're supposed to prefer, it's a rather sweet antidote to the pain and misery of daily life.

Lazy sex is a message to your partner that things don't have to always unfold like a porno movie or a romance novel. That you trust each other and are intimate enough to know how to just . . . do it.

This is something different from the "quickie," which has its place, too. This is more like a "barely." But like the quickie, it has its charms, and for couples who manage to defeat the tendency for sex to become as frequent as a Chicago Cubs World Series appearance, it is an essential part of the sexual repertoire.

Questions?

I'm tired of my boyfriend falling asleep right after we have sex. What should I do?

Let him sleep.

I've noticed this question sometimes appears in popular sex advice columns. And the answer the alleged expert gives involves your telling your boyfriend how much his sleeping upsets you, why he should be considerate and remain awake and cuddle, etc., etc. One writer even suggested giving him coffee an hour before doing the wild thing, so he'll be in a caffeine-induced frenzy the entire night! What's next, sprinkling crystal meth on his potato chips?

The truth is that most guys don't go to spas, they don't get massages, they don't vent their feelings to their friends or go to therapy. Most don't even work out. Since adolescence, they've had only one surefire method of relieving the tensions of life, and it's by having an orgasm.

Thus your average guy has trained himself to reach the deepest levels of relaxation right after the moment of climax. This was developed years before he met you, and it's no reflection on his love for you.

And, to be honest, if he likes sleeping with you, that in itself is a sign that he cares about you (or that you have a much nicer apartment). So if he expresses his love at all other times besides postcoitus, give the man a break and let him drift into sweet unconsciousness.

My friends and I are constantly debating how long you should date a guy before you have sex. You don't want to seem like a "ho" by doing it too soon, but on the other hand, a girl has needs!

The standard answer from writers of books like these is "wait till there's love," or "wait till you're engaged," or "wait till you're retired and living in Boca."

I think the amount of time a girl waits is dependent on upbringing, values, and social milieu. In the secular, competitive, anonymous, and hypersexual world of a large American city, women by and large will go to bed sooner than, say, women in a small religious community. No relationship writer is going to have an answer applicable to every reader.

Let me instead offer you some food for thought.

1. **It's Hard to Escape the Slut Zone**

Guys are much more enlightened about female sexuality than they were in the dark ages before fifteen-year-olds could watch *Sex and the City* and *understand every detail*. But however much men *acknowledge* that there's a double standard for women when it comes to sexual history, most men still prefer to settle down with a woman who's had fewer lovers than there are Billy Joel albums.

If you sleep with a guy on the first night, or not long

thereafter, you risk having that interpreted as a sign that you've done it many times before. This is a huge negative.

Now believe it or not, that way of looking at things might be unconsciously based on an important fact. One of the top predictors of whether a woman will cheat is the number of lovers she had before she got married. The higher the figure, the more likely she is to stray. The idea is that if a person has a taste for a variety of partners, that doesn't go away simply because she has a ring. I think guys intuitively recognize this, which is why their value of some chastity will always trump their politics.

2. **Sometimes You Just Know He's Right**

We're adults. We have the ability to make judgments, and to make exceptions for rules when the circumstances warrant it. Once or twice in your lifetime, you'll find that guy who you just *know* is someone special, with whom you share a special chemisty, who is more than good looks, and whom you know you must get naked with sooner than normal.

As a battle-hardened veteran of the dating scene, I've noticed that love is something that can emerge over time, but sexual chemistry is either there or it isn't. And when you feel that something special is in the air, when there's something electric between you and you've known each other long enough to develop some trust, sometimes you have to throw caution to the wind and let passion take over. (For some reason it's starting to sound like I'm writing copy for a Brazilian soap opera.)

What's up with guys wanting me to talk dirty? I never have any idea what to say.

Tell me about it. I dated this girl who wanted us to have phone sex, which, given that we both only had cell phones, was a complete farce because every other second I'd have to say, "What? I got the part about my balls, but I lost you till you said 'Like I'm the babysitter.'"

I'm also a paranoid. Even when I walk down the street I think I'm being videotaped, let alone when I'm naked and a girlfriend is asking me to call her a bad little girl. My assumption is whatever I say will end up on the Internet, probably on a loop with the latest celebrity sex video.

But I'm a neurotic person and you shouldn't emulate me.

Because many people love the dirty talk. So what's the harm in trying it? Assuming you know your man well enough to know whether he's activated a recording device, why not give it a go? It's not like he's looking for a Shakespearean level of eloquence; a good "I love how you [raunchy verb] my [name of sexy body part]" should suffice at first. Who knows? You might enjoy it.

My boyfriend is addicted to porn. He thinks he's clever because he clears the history on his Web browser, but I know how to look at the cookies to see where he's been. I'm too embarrassed to tell him I know, but he's making me nervous. What should I do?

Tell him it freaks you out, you Sherlock Holmes of the hard drive.

Having dark secrets pretty much defeats the purpose of being in a committed relationship, doesn't it? I once dated a girl for three months who I was convinced had breast implants. I wanted to ask her every day but I always chickened out. My whole lovemaking technique flew out the window as foreplay began to feature lengthy breast examinations. And it weighed on me because, for reasons I'll explain below, I never thought of myself as someone who'd settle down with someone who looks like she spends weekend nights working the champagne room.

One day I unburdened myself and asked her. When she stopped laughing at me, she said no, she owed her perfect, gravity-defying orbs to her mother. What a relief that was.

So you have a secret and the fact that it's tormenting you tells me you should bring it up, or you'll be as I was: insane.

But keep a couple of things in mind.

First, one website can generate numerous cookies, so he might be viewing less than you think. That means his "addiction" might not be an addiction at all. It might be ordinary, harmless, low-level male degeneracy.

Second, every study I've read suggests there's very little harm done by moderate porn viewing. It doesn't lead to rape. It doesn't lead to infidelity. It really just leads to additional credit card debt since these websites are notorious for adding phantom charges.

What's interesting is that if you asked guys who enjoy porn whether they'd like to *date or marry* a porn star, almost all of them say no. So it's not as if the women he sees are in any way your rivals: they're just fodder for his imagination, a way to vicariously experience the eternal male fantasy of sex with lots of willing women.

Just be nice and apologetic when you bring it up, as he will be totally humiliated and in search of a reason to change the subject.

I think my boyfriend is ashamed of his body because he always keeps a T-shirt on during sex. I wouldn't mind so much but one time it read, "I'm with Stupid."

Just pull his shirt off the next time things get going.

It's possible you'll have an after-school-special moment where he says, "I . . . I just don't want you to see . . . *my scar*." Or perhaps he has gynecomastia, aka man boobs, and his glands of shame will flop in front of you.

More likely he's either like me—i.e., has the pectorals of a nine-year-old—or he's overweight and looks pregnant. Either way, he doesn't reveal his substandard physique. The larger issue is that guys also have body image problems, though of course to a far less extent than do women.

But by just going for the shirt and pulling it off as if he's in a *Guys Gone Wild!* video, you'll either get the thing off once and for all, or he'll stop you and force some sort of discussion. And maybe it's my inner Richard Simmons talking, but I kind of like these talks where one person confesses his deepest insecurities and vulnerabilities.

Penis size. Your thoughts?

What hasn't already been said about this?

Whatever your guy has, that's it. There are no operations, no pills, no vacuum pumps, no fun-house mirrors that will change what nature provided. You know it. He knows it. You've both read all the ridiculous articles in *Cosmo* and on the Internet that have the headline "Size DOES Matter!" (As if anyone in history has ever thought it didn't.)

I suppose my only semi-original thought is that in several years of listening to people yammer about their relationship issues, not one woman has ever listed penis size as a criterion in her search for a man or as a reason for ending a relationship. In other words, when women explain why they're getting a divorce or breaking up with a long-term boyfriend, they'll say there's a lack of affection, communication, work ethic, sobriety, kindness, or intelligence—not "It's his dick."

So put this issue in the same category as a man's height. We know height matters, but many millions of short guys have made many millions of women very happy.

I've never enjoyed receiving oral sex. It makes me uncomfortable. But my boyfriend takes it really personally if I don't let him go down on me. He's really insistent about it, and I find it doesn't make the sex any better.

Many guys suffer from the "delivery boy" syndrome. They are so wrapped up in whether they're "delivering" the greatest sexual experience of your life that it becomes a distraction. That distraction makes you enjoy yourself less, which makes him try harder, which takes you both out of the moment and results in the problem I call You-Can't-Call-This-Serious-Compared-to-People-Suffering-in-Africa-but-It's-Nonetheless-a-Pain.

The first thing to deal with is the specific problem of your not liking to receive oral. There are therapists who will tell you this is a reflection of deeper problems of intimacy, your relationship with your grandmother, how society bamboozles women into ignorance about the clitoris, etc., etc.

I, however, don't think it's the end of the world if a person's sexual tastes don't conform to the model of sexual likes and dislikes that happens to be the standard of the day. You don't like oral. You might simply need to ask your partner to not do it because it's not your thing.

Now because your boyfriend wants so much to please you, you need to make it clear that you can still be taken to the stars sexually without oral sex. That's hard for most enlightened males to believe, but if it's true, let him know so he won't feel like he can't be the lover he wants to be.

Look. I know millions of guys suffer from premature ejaculation. And I don't want to hurt my boyfriend's feelings. BUT HE COMES IN LIKE THIRTY SECONDS. What should I do?

Most guys have a solution to this problem. It's called "no longer being a teenager." Others endure indescribable anxiety, self-doubt, and humiliation because of it, well into middle age and beyond.

But if I may turn the clock back to being seventeen years old. . .

You, female reader, have no idea what a guy who has PE goes through.

The fear starts around the time you sense that the girl is actually going to let you go all the way. Until then, you've become extraordinary at kissing, massaging, and other elements of foreplay, much in the manner of a blind person whose hearing has become highly refined to compensate for the absence of vision.

The big night arrives. By then you've developed techniques. Perhaps you've masturbated once or twice just to get an ejaculation out of your system. Maybe you've brought a pack of those sense-deadening condoms. Or maybe you're just praying that this time it'll be different.

Then the moment arrives and . . . it's over before it started. You have your BS lines that you use to cover yourself—this has never happened before, it's only because you're so hot, etc.—but somehow you both know it's untrue.

Your suspicions are confirmed when it happens again. And again.

The only saving grace, at least if you're under age twenty-five, is that if you came once at, say midnight, you might get another erection at 12:05. And THAT erection is golden because it'll last FOREVER if you want it to. Of course this presumes that the girl hasn't kicked you out, or that you haven't fled in defeat.

The point is that PE is no fun.

So in a second I'm going to suggest he start reading books and talking to professionals. But in the interest of honesty, I'll share a tip. If he's young, try giving him a chance at a second round. Also, you can say that you want him to give you extended oral after he prematurely climaxes. That way he feels like he's doing his job as a man, and you can enjoy yourself in the process.

Also, to guys reading this, sometimes the cause is how

you do things when you're alone. If you grew up with lots of siblings, chances are you used your tiny moments of privacy to masturbate as quickly as possible, and inadvertently trained yourself to be too quick. You may be able to reverse this process by training yourself to take more time and think distracting thoughts as you approach climax.

Now. I've made lots of fun of therapists, but this is one problem where professional help may be the best thing. But that's something he'll have to find out for himself, and he's more likely to invest the money in it if it seems like you'll stick with him through the process.

We have the opposite problem. He lasts forever. I end up getting bored and/or very dry.

Doctors have a term for this: retarded ejaculation. I personally feel it should be called mentally challenged ejaculation, but that's an argument for another day.

Most guys have it every now and then. Maybe we've drunk too much, maybe we're scared, who knows. The point is that it puts guys in the ridiculous position of having to fake orgasm because we know the girl will suspect something is amiss if we just end things by saying, "Well, that's it for me!"

But if it's a persistent problem, there might be physiological causes for it, so he should see a doctor.

And on that note, let me bring to your attention . . .

10 THINGS
THE MEN OF AMERICA
HOPE YOU WILL REMEMBER

1. Although there is a male sexual nature and a female sexual nature, we are united in our desire to pull each other's clothes off.

2. Men feel enormous pressure to "perform" in bed.

3. Men *want* to please you, if only for the ego-gratifying desire to be the best.

4. Lazy sex will increase your frequency of sex and bring you happiness even if it sounds preposterous. Try it this week with someone you love and report your findings to me.

5. It's actually a compliment if your guy falls asleep after sex: he feels the relationship is intimate enough for him to completely relax with you.

6. If you're debating whether to sleep with a guy sooner or later, I always suggest later.

7. It's not the end of the world if you don't like receiving oral sex. Just look into whether it's because you might in some way be uncomfortable with yourself or your partner.

8. Avoid fakery. Men are more turned on by a quiet performance that's real than a loud one that's not.

9. Don't despair. Premature ejaculation is curable.

10. "Retarded ejaculation." Who thinks of these names?

She's the One:
In His Own Words

thought it might be fun to end this book with the question that began it: What makes a guy think of a woman as a keeper?

You're about to read the answers as given by some of the guys I interviewed for this book. But keep this in mind: you're not getting the sanitized, women's-magazine version. In other words, some of what these guys say doesn't exactly have the eloquence of Lord Byron. (I'm thinking of the guy, not included here, who said he knew his girlfriend was the One when she "acted all sweet and shit.") But have a heart. Guys aren't used to expressing this kind of stuff. Try to see through the mangled language to the sincerity beneath it.

We begin with David.

David
The Handsome Twenty-Seven-Year-Old
Married Guy

David lives in New Jersey AND IS INCREDIBLY GOOD-LOOKING. Like Tom Cruise with an eight dollar haircut, this guy is. He and his wife, Lisa, have been married for two years.

GG: So when did you know?

DAVID: I can point to the exact, specific moment because my wife and I got engaged after only seven months. We were in a Bennigan's in Delaware. And there was this guy in the bar we knew who was graduating from college. And he was all upset and bothered about his life. Really depressed. Sitting at a bar, washing away his tears into a pint.

GG: Okay.

DAVID: And he's all like, "I can't believe I'm going into the real world and picking something I'll do the rest of my life." It's like he's feeling like he's on death row. So Lisa says, "Why? Why does there have to be the one thing you do for the rest of your life? Why can't you just do this, try it out, see what it's like, and if not, you can al-

ways change. If you really think you can't change, you
might as well die right now."

GG: At Bennigan's.

DAVID: And that to me was like the seal, even though it had
only been a couple of months that we were together. I
knew there was something there that was really special.

GG: Go on.

DAVID: It was something I never heard before. I was like,
"Wow, this is somebody I better hold on to." Because it
was different from anything I'd ever seen. Different from
anything I'd ever heard.

GG: Imagine the reader wondering what the hell you're
talking about.

DAVID: It was the fact that she was so open-minded. That she
thought that you can do anything you want. We'd been
having a good time dating and everything. The sex was
great. But when she was talking to that guy—it was inspiring. It was an inspiring moment. Anybody who can
do that and light up—she's like a firefly. A firefly in a lot
of ways.

GG: You're on a roll.

DAVID: She lights up. She just lights up. She's smart, she's funny,
and I love that. She can hang with anyone, intelligence-
wise. In conversation.

GG: That's fantastic.

DAVID: I was with a girl before that who was depressed all the time. And once a week we'd have sex, and she was fine then, but all the other times she was upset and depressed and annoyed. The last thing you want is somebody who's going to pull you down all the time.

GG: You want a firefly.

DAVID: That's right.

Tom
The Forty-Two-Year-Old Divorced Gangsta

Tom is a guy's guy. He lives in Queens, New York. He drives a black SUV. He wears white tank tops and smokes cigars. He looks like an extra from the movie *Goodfellas*. He's tough, you know what I mean? That is, until he starts talking about his thirty-three-year-old girlfriend, Diane.

GG: So Tom. When did you know Diane was the one?

TOM: I don't know if I can put my finger on a specific day or moment that really made that clear to me.

GG: Well, help me out here because I'm trying to write a book.

TOM: [Laughs] Well, I think that women tend to go from, like, there's "dating" and then there's "I kind of like him" to "I could stay with him forever." I think that I acted really sort of feminine about the whole thing. [Laughs] I just knew right away she was the one.

GG: Speak more.

TOM: When I started seeing Diane, when I hung out with her the first time, it really was a defining moment that made me realize I cared about her. It's almost like, from the very beginning I wanted to be with her. It wasn't how she flipped her hair, or some opinion, and that's when I said, "Oh my God! She's the one!" It was weird. From the very first time we went out, I was very close to her.

GG: But there must have been something about her. Was it just the chemistry between you two?

TOM: I'd say it's the friendship. It's the ability to hang out with someone after having sex. Because men are very weird like that. Guys will have sex with a woman. And it's after they have sex, is when they discover their friendship. Prior to sex, they're fogged by this, "Oh, I love hanging out with you!" And everything she says, you're like, "You're a genius!" And you agree with her.

GG: But that doesn't last.

TOM: What I really appreciate, what it comes down to, is companionship and friendship. How I know she loves me, and how there's that support and that love. I could just sense that goodness right away. That's what deep down a guy—a person—really wants.

GG: And you must have been right because you've been to-gether for years.

TOM: Yeah. Because the sex in the beginning? That's bull-shit. What's going to keep a relationship together is *talk-ing about your day*. If you can't do that, there's nothing. Remember: if you're an asshole, you're still going to be a dick.

GG: Well said. I think.

Alex

The Twenty-Four-Year-Old Hipster Who Wears Cool T-Shirts and Attracts Brainy Girls

I don't understand these young hipsters today, what with their haircuts borrowed from the Monkees and their disdain for . . . everything. But there are so many of them that I felt obligated to interview one.

GG: When did you know?

ALEX: It's an involved story.

GG: I have time, believe me.

ALEX: I was living here in New York the summer between my junior and senior years in college [at the University of Toronto]. And I met her at the Coney Island *Village*

Voice music thing they have every year. And I wasn't serious about meeting someone there.

GG: It's hot, everyone is talking about how they hate the Strokes. . . .

ALEX: If you've ever been to one of these things, there's tons of hipster girls. And they're all pretty hot. But she really stood out. Because she's funkier than that. I was like, "Wow. I gotta make my move."

GG: Let's get to the emotional part.

ALEX: In a larger sense, my feelings for her had to do with how she went out on a limb emotionally for me. That she *showed how she was falling in love with me.* Which is a huge confidence booster. And there were two things that really did that. One was that when we first met, she gave me her phone number.

GG: Nice.

ALEX: And I called her, and she didn't return my call. And I thought, because we'd had this incredible day together, "She's the one who got away."

GG: Which is the opposite of what we're talking about.

ALEX: Right. But I suddenly get an email from her, like two weeks later, and she said, "I think you're the right person, because I Googled 'Alex + the University of Toronto.'" She didn't know my last name.

GG: That's a lot of people.

ALEX: So she found my column in my school paper to get my email address. I was like, "Wow. She really wants to get together." That said that "Wow, this is going to work out." It was kind of an electrifying moment, even though it was over email.

GG: You said there was a second thing.

ALEX: So then we went out. And she's an artist, and we went to an exhibit at the Whitney Museum. And it was clear that she wasn't fucked up.

GG: Which when you're talking about artists, is unusual.

ALEX: Right. She was very intelligent and could speak about anything art-related. And I feel kind of dumb about art. I was like, "I just enjoy the painting," and she was able to dig my simple pleasure of enjoying art, but then she could get deep and intellectual about it. I kept thinking, "Wow. I haven't met someone like you before."

GG: So I think what you're saying is . . .

ALEX: That for me, at the highest level, what a guy wants is that comfort, is that knowing a girl really wants you, that you just know you're going to be together every week-end, and that you don't always have to be impressive every second you're with her.

GG: Some people call that love.

ALEX: That's right. Guys want love. I can't believe I said that.

Omar
The Thirty-Two-Year-Old Graphic Designer

Omar is the last guy on earth you'd think would get engaged. He's good-looking, successful, and had a single life that isn't done justice by the word "active." Then he met his fiancée, Stacey, and everything changed.

GG: I think you know the question.

OMAR: I don't know if there was a eureka moment where I realized she's the one.

GG: So it was gradual.

OMAR: Over time I just noticed myself being more of an idiot around her. I think we all have an inner moron, and we feel like when we're around a girl we have to suppress it so you can seem cool.

GG: Example of your inner moron?

OMAR: I do bathroom opera.

GG: Nice.

OMAR: [Laughing] Yeah. I'll make an aria out of going to the bathroom. She laughs. I feel like I can be myself. That's so important. I guess you could say that's when I knew.

GG: Sometimes women tell me that they think guys only care about looks.

OMAR: Looks are packaging. You got to market the T & A. But it's like the design on a Coke can or something.

GG: Go on.

OMAR: It can't be the basis of the next sixty years of your life. You're looking for a Thelma and Louise situation. You're just—you're traveling through life.

GG: Traveling is important to you.

OMAR: My dream is to travel the world. One day Stacey and I were looking at the paper and there was this travel article on Morocco. She said, "Why don't we pick up and go live in Morocco?" At that point I realized she wasn't just a great woman that I loved, but someone I could travel the world with.

GG: What about how she gets along with your family?

OMAR: Every guy has this idea about what being married is like. Part of that is he has this wife who knows how to make his mom happy.

GG: Does Stacey do that?

OMAR: Oh yeah.

GG: You're getting married soon, so tell the readers what surprise you have planned. I must say it's very romantic.

OMAR: I'm taking her on a secret honeymoon. She doesn't know where we're going. I stole her passport and told her, "After we're married, you'll find out where we're going."

GG: I assume it's somewhere nice.

OMAR: It's beautiful.

GG: Can you tell us where?

OMAR: I'm not telling anyone. You'll have to put it in the next edition.

Dawson

The Twenty-Nine-Year-Old Sensitive Guy

Dawson works for public radio. He wears corduroy blazers with jeans. Worries about the environment. Speaks softly. Has a great sense of humor. The ladies love him, not just because he's funny and self-effacing and knows Ira Glass, but because he is ONE OF THE NICEST GUYS EVER TO INHABIT PLANET EARTH.

GG: So when did you know she was the one?

DAWSON: Can I answer it in a roundabout way?

GG: Sure.

DAWSON: I've sometimes found—and I think it probably happens to everybody after they've dated people for a certain period of time—that there's a kind of sediment of former relationships that you bring to new ones, based on things about other people that have hurt you.

GG: Don't get too fancy on me now.

DAWSON: [Laughs] Well, with Abigail, there's been certain

163

instances where I've found myself preemptively apologizing for mistakes I thought I was making.

GG: Can you give an example?

DAWSON: There was a night where she asked me to go out with her and a friend, but at the last minute I couldn't go out, or I made plans I forgot about. The next time I talked to her I felt kind of awkward and was stumbling over an apology.

GG: As we all do at times.

DAWSON: Right. And this happened two or three times, but each time it became clear that this wasn't an issue *for her at all*. She's just so easy about it. Everything I think is going to be a huge problem, she's like, "That's okay. It's not a big deal." Or she makes a joke out of it.

GG: Tell the readers why that was so important to you.

DAWSON: I just think that that side of her personality just opened up the idea on an emotional level for me that I could really stay with her for a long time.

GG: Because fighting is that big a deal.

DAWSON: It is. Now that might sound like I want somebody who's kind of a doormat. That's not what I'm saying. Actually conflict on some level—intellectual disagreement and conversations—is great.

GG: It's the soul-crushing grind of needless arguing you hate.

DAWSON: [Laughs] I can live without the fireworks. Or if there are fireworks, that they're jovial fireworks.

GG: And she's a firefly.

DAWSON: Excuse me?

Jimmy
The Thirty-Four-Year-Old Chef

Jimmy is the owner/chef of an upscale Greek restaurant. He's the kind of guy who can bend a kitchen full of guys to his will, but also be quiet and reflective when speaking of matters of the heart. He's lived with his girlfriend, Mia, for five years.

GG: If it's not too awkward, tell me about falling in love with Mia.

JIMMY: This is awkward.

GG: You're right. But let's try to get through it.

JIMMY: [Laughing] Well, you know I love to go out to the clubs. I love the whole trappings—the celebrities, the bottle service, the music, the whole scene.

GG: I've heard of these things.

JIMMY: We're at this place, and all my friends are with us, and Mia says to me, "I'd like to go home with you now." It wasn't a sexual thing. It was like she was saying, "I don't need any of this to enjoy being with you."

GG: And you . . .

JIMMY: In that split second I realized, I was like, "Of course.

There *is* nothing here for me." I didn't need the crazy nights out. I didn't need the single life. I just needed someone I could be happy with at home.

GG: That's the goal.

JIMMY: For guys, it's like there's looks at first, but then it's all about laughing in the morning. That you have jokes that are funny only to the two of you. Then there's a bigger step. The way the girl makes you feel about yourself. She opened my eyes to all of that.

GG: What do you mean?

JIMMY: There's a kind of love where you feel that you're a better person because of her. That because of her you want to do better. Because she's in your life, it's like you want to focus on your career to provide for her.

GG: I think I'm going to do a whole chapter on why guys want a woman who makes them feel successful.

JIMMY: That's crucial. Every guy has that sense of insecurity, and this lack of self-worth.

GG: Explain.

JIMMY: For me, I left a really good job to open this restaurant at the age of thirty-two. For all I know it'll be some tragic disaster. I have this nightmare that one day she'll wake up and decide to marry an investment banker. But she's always telling me, "I'm with you as long as you want to do this." To have a woman who supports you is a very big deal. It gives you strength.

GG: Definitely.

JIMMY: When a woman acts with true selflessness, I think it makes men think about her in a different way. It forces you, right or wrong, to think of her in a serious way because you're like, "This is an amazing person." That's the moment he's going to think about being with you long-term.

GG: Any other thoughts?

JIMMY: When you think about someone you love, it's never about the big event, or that night we went to that crazy diner, or when we went skydiving or something. You think back to real dumb stuff, like reading the paper, or joking together, or just being happy together one afternoon. I don't know what that represents, but that's when you think about someone you love.

GG: The sweet boredom achieved only with a girl you love.

JIMMY: Exactly.

We've reached the end of the line. I hope you've had fun. And I hope you have a feeling of optimism. There's a guy out there waiting to feel that special "click" that tells him you're not just another date. That you're someone incredibly special he never wants to lose. And I hope that as he's feeling that, you're feeling it, too. That deep down, you've decided he's the one.

Bonus Chapter

How to Meet a Decent Guy in the First Place

I finished the following chapter not sure it belonged in this book. But then it occurred to me that single people are usually happy to hear ideas about how to meet someone new, so here are my thoughts. The chapter starts with my reaction to speed dating, and ends with a fancy chart.

The bald guy doesn't have a chance. You can see it on his face.

The girl at Table D is a superstar; you have to pry the men out of the seat across from her. But there is disappointment in her eyes, too. At least four of the folks look far, far older than the maximum age of forty. The hostess is so young and so pretty and so indifferent to the misery before her that her presence exacerbates the agony of it all.

Welcome to a night of speed dating, Manhattan-style.

It's a Tuesday night and I'm taking notes at the bar of a downtown club called Sutra. In the back, sixteen women sit against the banquettes. Each has a card on her table with a letter of the alphabet on it. Every four minutes the hostess blows a whistle, and the sixteen guys scurry—or fail to scurry, if they are at Table D—to the next woman.

I have been given permission to attend this event by the folks at HurryDate.com. Their very nice PR person no doubt expects me to do what every other relationship writer does when attending these events: have a few drinks on the company's tab, then basically rewrite their press release (i.e., "A great way to meet Mr. Right if you're pressed for time!").

But I can't.

Speed dating might have been started with good intentions—it's the brainchild of Yaacov Deyo, a Rabbi who wanted to encourage Jewish singles to meet one another. But years later, separated from its noble origins, it has morphed into something to be enjoyed only by masochists and *perhaps even Satan himself.*

What do I mean? We'll get to that in a minute. Just as we'll discuss online dating, how what you do for a living and where you live can profoundly change your romantic opportunities, what courses and political groups can put you in the orbit of available guys, and what I mean when I urge you to exploit the *Babylon 5* Principle.

But first a confession.

If there were a secret to how to meet the perfect guy, I'd share it, and in the process sell more books than if Dan Brown and J. K. Rowling published *The Harry Potter–Da Vinci Code Diet!* But there is no secret. Meeting a guy for more than just sex is, and probably always has been, a task that requires strategy. That's what I'm offering here: a few principles and tactics for increasing your odds. I'd also like to cut through some of the nonsense that's been written in praise of bad ideas. Let's begin with something obvious.

Avoid Speed Dating

An objective for anyone looking for a boyfriend or girl-friend should be to *run from social situations that replicate high school.* Remember high school? Everyone had a crush on the same three people. The most popular three people. And why these people were so popular, the reason they were held in such esteem and inspired crushes in their underlings, were, in order: looks, looks, and looks.

Ranking in high school has little to do with intelligence and good values, and has everything to do with what we're told we should discount, especially if we are looking for a long-term relationship.

Speed Dating = Ninth Grade

Speed dating mimics high school. Your interrogator, as he sits across from you for all of 240 seconds, is not interested in your soul. He is sizing up your looks and ranking you against the other women. It's a competitive, cutthroat environment.

Now as speed dating events progress, you check on a small form who you want to meet. And invariably, the same three people of each sex are selected by the entire group. You are set up with them only if they have also checked you.

The entire time you are on your "date," you are conscious of being judged in these harsh terms, and this can lead to all kinds of errors and embarrassments. A worker for HurryDate told me one guy was so nervous he confessed to being molested! (Of course I had to laugh when I imagined him saying, "And then . . . he put his hand on my leg and—" *Ding!* Times up!)

Education, a desire to start family, kindness—these traits don't mean jack in speed dating. What matters to guys is how thin the women are. To women, it's mainly the guy's facial attractiveness, his height, and whether he has a decent physique. It makes us much more shallow than we naturally are.

Sounds fun, right?

Science

Don't just take my word for it.

In 2005, Robert Kurzban of the University of Pennsylvania published a study called "HurryDate: Mate Preferences in Action." In it, he and his colleague Jason Weeden analyzed data from 10,526 participants in HurryDate sessions. Some excerpts from the study:

- ". . . HurryDate participants are given three minutes in which to make their judgments, but they mostly could be made in three seconds."

- ". . . the attributes that predicted women's desirability at HurryDate events were physically observable ones."

- ". . . the primary predictors of men's desirability were higher facial attractiveness, taller stature, younger age, [and] closer to the middle (25) BMI."

Confirmation

Just to make sure I understood his study, I called Dr. Kurzban.

"So would Arthur Miller have a chance with Marilyn Monroe in this situation?" I asked. "I mean, he's a genius, but he's hideous compared to her, so if what he has to offer is his mind, would he do okay in a HurryDate environment?"

"Not really," said the good professor.

From which I draw this conclusion.

There's nothing wrong with taking a chance, especially when you are, in theory, meeting around twenty new guys in an hour. The problem is that it's not just you who's meeting those guys. It's you and nineteen other women. So the same guy who'd like you if he worked with you, or if he heard about you from a friend and went to lunch with you, might, when presented with someone he thinks is hotter, take a pass on you. And, likely, that woman will take a pass on him. The only winner is the company to which you paid the registration fee.

But if you still want to give it a shot, bring a friend. Think of it as something you're doing so you can go out for drinks afterward and laugh about it.

Imagine the jokes you'll make about the guys as they're speaking to you. Try to have fun, but don't spend money on it unless it's easy to spare.

Just don't get your hopes up.

Online Dating
Get the Monster to Work for You

Imagine you're a guy.

Since the age of thirteen, you've spent most of your life thinking about girls. Where to meet girls. How to talk to girls. What career would most impress girls, whether you're handsome enough for girls, if you will ever find another girl to have sex with you. Your priorities change as you get older—love and companionship become as important as sex, for example—but no matter what state of life you've reached, if you're single (and, for some guys, even if you're not), at some base level, you're still a foraging, prehistoric male in perennial search of a new female, and your desire has almost no limits.

Which brings me to Internet dating, and why it's so screwed up.

Too Much

When your average guy browses through the profiles of, say, Match.com, his senses are overwhelmed. There, before him, is *a gallery of available women*!!! Tall women! Short women! Blond women! Asian/Hispanic/African-American/Alaskan-Native women! Uzbek midgets, if he so desires!

He can check off a few boxes in the search form, press Submit, and BAM! There's another twenty-five photos of fantastic, not-so-fantastic, but available *girls*. And none of them know what a loser he is! Why, it is perfectly possible to email them all, change his profile to add a few tens of thousands of dollars to his income, use Photoshop to paste hair to his head, lie about wanting a serious relationship, and meet them all! Not every guy has this reaction, but many do.

This means that a reasonable, quality girl in search of a reasonable, quality guy must hack through a thicket of deceit, mediocrity, and bad intentions if she wishes to meet a guy online. And don't tell me networking sites like Friendster or MySpace are any different; guys prowl around them as much as they do Yahoo! and Match.com—they just happen to have been born during the Reagan administration.

Taming the Monster: Seven Tips

Despite these drawbacks, online dating offers a phenomenal opportunity to meet someone new. After all, according to a study quoted by the *Wall Street Journal*, it's the way nearly two million Americans have met their spouses. It's just that the objective, from the outset, has to be *to locate a hidden gem*. Or to recognize one when he sends you an email and a link to his profile. I'll give you some tactics for doing just that, but first let's go over some rules of thumb.

1. **Never Establish Intimacy Through Email.** There is no greater cause of heartache than this. None. A guy sends you his profile, you start exchanging emails, and somehow the literary flourish of his emails has you more smitten than Michael Jackson at a Chuck E. Cheese. (Bad joke, sorry.) The truth is that email, however useful it may be for work and/or penis enlargement ads, is unable to accurately convey emotional content between strangers. And it in no way replicates how two people will react when they see each other. Which brings me to the next rule . . .

2. **Make Dates, Not Phone Calls.** Phone calls are not unlike emails. They can foster a fake relationship based on only tiny aspects of who two people really are. Put another way: some guys are great on the phone but are horrendous in person.

3. **Be Wary of Personality Tests.** Certain online dating services offer personality tests. Some of these tests take longer than the average human lifespan to complete, but that's another story. The problem is that none of these tests is as accurate or comprehensive as the best test of all: sitting down, looking a person in the eye, and judging him for yourself. The point is, if you're using, say, eHarmony to meet someone, that's great. Just be aware that even if they say someone is your perfect match, you really won't

know if you like him until you see him and talk to him. In person.

4. **Don't Over-Date.** It's tempting to act like a guy, especially if much of your life has been a very long dating dry spell. But if you're going out on three or four dates per week with three or four different guys, your goal is to acquire a self-esteem boost, not a boyfriend.

5. **Don't Date Photographers.** This is a personal, petty judgment of mine based on the misery of my female friends. Feel free to ignore it. But from what I've seen, guys who are photographers—and I'm thinking more of the types who hit on models than those who look for sunsets and waterfalls—always manage, through their photographic trickery, to make themselves look better than they actually look, and have chosen their trade to prey on women's vanity *for the purpose of getting laid*. In other words, when a guy says he's a "photographer," substitute the phrase "in a band in order to get more sex" and see if you're still interested.

6. **Avoid Anyone Looking for a "Casual Relationship."** Very likely these folks are also looking for a "cure for herpes."

7. **Avoid Guys Who Talk About Sex Too Soon.** My friend Sophia, whom you met in the jealousy chapter, recently told me that back when she was registered for Match.com,

a guy sent her a profile in which he'd drawn an ejaculating penis with the asterisk key. Now. There are guys out there who think this is a good idea, just as there are guys who will start chatting about sex in their emails and IMs. I think this is an early warning that they have no sense of self-control. A guy who wants a girlfriend understands that online dating is merely an updated means of courting a woman. He knows he has to make an effort to be charming, smart, etc. A guy who cuts right to the chase with the dirty talk hasn't learned this elementary lesson of male/female interaction, and that is a sign he must be deleted. Figuratively.

Finding a Hidden Gem . . . on the Internet!

Think of the guy you'd like to marry.

Is he the type of guy who'd get a professional head shot for an online profile? Would he spend hours and hours fine-tuning his mini essay, developing perfectly witty missives to mass email to the women he wants to meet, join multiple dating services, and list "any/any/any/any" in his criteria for the woman he wants to meet? Would he even be on an Internet dating site in the first place?

If you answered no to any of the above, keep reading.

Some of the best guys have the worst profiles. No photo. No activity in more than three weeks. A mini essay that has glimmers of intelligence and humor but isn't too polished. Why would any of these guys be worth sending a note to? Because the reason they have crappy profiles might be that (1) they aren't players, or (2) they have jobs in which they are managers or teachers or otherwise have high visibility and would be humiliated if anyone knew they were looking for love online.

It goes without saying that most of the guys with awful profiles, just like the ones with terrific profiles, aren't the ones for you. But I think it's worth taking a chance. It's even worth breaking one of the aforementioned rules—that you shouldn't spend too much time emailing before going on a date. You don't have a ton to go on, so it's worthwhile to ask him to send you a photo (and ALWAYS do this right away), find out what he does for a living, and see whether there's more to him than the shadowy "No Photo Available" he presents online.

Keywords

One of the things I like about Match.com is that you can keyword search. A terrific way to narrow the field if, say, education is important to you is to enter the name of a good school and see what you get. Enter "Columbia" and you'll get a bunch of Ivy League graduates. And if their snobbery bothers you, fear not, because you will also get people who don't know how to spell the name of the country. The same idea applies if you like to travel. Enter "skiing" and not only will you get guys looking for cocaine pals, but you might find someone who shares your interest in winter sports AND who has money.

First Dates

One last thought on online dating. Where and when you meet someone for the first time is critical to whether the relationship gets off on the right foot AND to your peace of mind.

Here's what I mean.

Most people arrange midafternoon meetings at a place like Starbucks. (There are some of you who will meet a stranger in his apartment; it goes without saying you should NEVER go to a guy's place, or invite him to yours, until you really know him.) But is there any place less sexy than a brightly lit chain coffeehouse filled with eavesdroppers? The moment you meet someone there, everyone knows what you're up to. It's inhibiting and faintly pathetic.

This is why I urge you to *meet on a weeknight at a nice bar or lounge near where you live, and be sure to arrive early*. Let's see why.

1. **Arrive early.** The rationale is simple. You want to know how tall a guy is. If *he* arrives first, and he remains seated when you make contact and stays seated when you leave, you will depart wondering.

2. **Stay near where you live.** There is nothing worse than having a horrendous date AND having to take a long drive home, pay thirty dollars for a taxi, take a flight, etc. You're also more comfortable on your home turf.

3. **Meet at a nice bar or lounge.** Every city has at least one of these. The idea is that you'll both look your best, and you'll be in an environment that feels more like a date than a business appointment. Unlike at Starbucks, there will be no one screaming, "Double soy mocha chai latte!" every three seconds. There will not be annoying teenagers swarming around you, and there will not be some creepy guy looking at porn on his laptop at the next table. You will have all the time-honored elements of good chemistry: darkness, alcohol, and privacy. Also, there is none of the pressure of a fancy dinner, or any other date that would require more than thirty minutes of your life. You can end it quickly and get home if necessary.

4. **Make it a weeknight.** Do this for a few reasons. First, since most guys you meet from the Internet will be duds, there is no reason to sacrifice a weekend night to someone you'll never date again. Second, bars and lounges tend to be packed on weekends, which means it'll be hard to talk and hard to find a table. There's also something to be said for making a guy think you're so busy you can only spare

a Tuesday night. Being desirable has always had something to do with seeming unavailable, and confessing that your calendar is completely blank can turn guys off.

This brings us to the final section of our tutorial. . . .

The *Babylon 5* Principle

Have you ever watched the Sci-Fi Channel? If so, you may have stumbled across the interstellar epic *Babylon 5*.

Babylon 5 is known for several things, one of which is that its fans make *Star Trek* nerds like me look fashionable and cool. Were you to attend a *Babylon 5* convention, you would find guys who have the hipness of a young Bill Gates. You would also find yourself one of the few women there, and irrespective of your looks, you would be the belle of the ball.

I'm being mean and snarky but there's an underlying principle here: the laws of supply and demand govern relations between the sexes as much as they govern the price of real estate. A mediocre guy in an environment of women— say, in a ballet class—will have a much easier time finding an attractive girlfriend than if he were in a male-dominated physics class. A woman who's attractive and a social worker or an elementary school teacher has a harder time having a love life than an attractive woman who's a police officer. Why? Because police departments are filled with guys and elementary schools are not. The odds are in her favor.

Should I go on? Think of New York City or Los Angeles. Every day, all over the world, smart, beautiful women decide they can gain the most advantage from their talents by moving to these two cities. But the fact that so many act on this idea ends up sabotaging their goals. The supply of these women is so high that the love life or career they could have had in, say, Chicago would have been far, far superior to what they end up with.

A Personal Example

I have a female friend who, at this moment, is the toast of a certain town in Iowa where there's a famous graduate writing program. She has a terrific, good-looking boyfriend. For years she worked in fashion in New York, but couldn't get a date even if, in her words, "I walked down the street naked with a sign offering free sex and a wide-screen TV." The reason? Her life here was a world of gay men and other women.

Iowa is her *Babylon 5* convention. This is not a slight against Iowa—it's actually a compliment: there are proportionally more good guys out there than there are in New York City. Guys in New York aren't *bad*; there are just fewer of us. You've heard this a million times if you've ever seen

Sex and the City; it's pretty much the only conversation single women have in New York.

Science

I know we just went over online dating, and to read all the press it gets, you'd think it was how every couple in America first met. The truth is that most people meet through friends, through family, at work, or at school. According to a 2005 survey by Princeton University, when asked "How did you and your current spouse/partner first meet," a sample of 3,215 Americans gave these answers:

39%	At work or school
35%	Through friends or family
13%	At a nightclub, bar or café, or other social gathering
3%	Church
1%	By chance/On the street
1%	Live in same neighborhood
1%	At a recreation facility
1%	Blind date/Dating service
*	Grew up together
4%	Miscellaneous other
3%	Don't know/Refused

This is a sample of the entire population, not just people with bachelor's degrees. Only 29 percent of American adults have a four-year college degree, and I'm guessing that because these people are more inclined to move somewhere new, or to have Internet access, the numbers would be higher for both "At a nightclub, bar or café, or other social gathering" and "Blind date/Dating service."

But friends, family, work, and school would still be the main sources of finding spouses. My point is that you should use the *Babylon 5* Principle to best take advantage of these environments.

Where the Boys Are

What sorts of professions, classes, and cities do guys gravitate toward? In a second you can read the handy chart I've created. But first a caveat. I'm certainly not urging you to drop everything, move to Baltimore, and take a trigonometry course just to meet men. I guess I'm saying that there will be opportunities in your life to do something, or visit someplace, and the fact that so many couples get their start through personal networking, jobs, or school means that if this opportunity will put you squarely in the realm of tons of guys, why not go for it?

When I was single and doing stand-up comedy, if someone told me to take a magazine journalism class, I'd have laughed. But having since taken magazine journalism classes, I now know that the world of publishing is a gold mine of brilliant, funny, attractive women.

So enjoy the chart and go forth, making friends and meeting guys.

And in moments of difficulty, always remember: whatever you're doing to meet a guy, it's better than speed dating.

	Girls Like . . .	**Boys Like . . .**
Professions	• Media and Entertainment • Medicine • Law • Advertising • Teaching • Nonprofits	• Any job that involves carrying a gun • Trading in stocks and bonds, and saying that they are "trading in stocks and bonds" • Putting out fires • Being called "doctor," even if they are mere PhDs
College Majors	• Humanities • Social Sciences • Education • Social Work • Psychology • Anything followed by the word "Studies" or preceded by the word "Creative"	• If they are athletes, anything that doesn't require attendance • Philosophy • Sciences • Math • Engineering • Falling into Jägermeister-induced coma
Countries in Which to Find People Who Want to Have Sex with You	• Italy • Greece • France • Jamaica • Any place where *Sex and the City* is on television and the women wear veils	• Any economically moribund nation in Eastern Europe • Asia (all of it)
Places of Leisure	• Home • Dance clubs • Places in which they are unlikely to be murdered	• Bars in which there are more televisions than patrons • Bars in which the bathroom may have been condemned by the CDC

Photo by Kristin Hoebermann

ABOUT THE AUTHOR

Gregory Gilderman has been giving frank and humorous relationship advice for so long he has considered changing his name to "Dr. Greg, Unlicensed Therapist." His column, The Dating Life, reaches nearly one million readers in *Metro* newspapers in Boston, Philadelphia, and New York, and he is a frequent contributor to *Cosmopolitan* and other women's magazines. His cable talk show, *Mr. Greg Live*, aired in New York from 2001 to 2004, and you can enjoy his amusing yet insightful advice program on his website, www.DoctorGreg.tv.